SERVE ONE
finding joy in serving others

by Tony Wolf

To Anthony
Serve Him
with your life!
Tony
James 1:27

Skye Books

ISBN: 0692485473
ISBN 13: 9780692485477
Library of Congress Control Number: 2015912830
LCCN Imprint Name: CreateSpace Independent Publishing Platform, North Charleston, SC

For Brooklyn, Katie, Adrienne, and Jude: The greatest joy you will ever know is serving others.

Contents

Foreword

I met Tony Wolf when he was our speaker on The Rock & Worship Roadshow tour. My band started Roadshow to feature the best Christian musicians together on one stage for a tour of twenty or so cities. The lineup has featured artists like Skillet, Third Day, Jeremy Camp, LeCrae, and Rend Collective, with MercyMe headlining each year.

Each night, we asked Tony to share about a ministry we have long been a part of—Compassion International. Compassion is a Christian child-advocacy ministry that releases children from spiritual, economic, social, and physical poverty and enables them to become responsible, fulfilled Christian adults. Tony's presentation was incredibly effective. It takes a big personality to command the attention of an arena in the midst of a ten-band concert. Tony seemed to do this effortlessly, night after night. Yes, he is a funny guy. And, yes, he is a superb communicator. That said, there is an incredibly rare, authentic transparency about Tony when he shares his story and delivers the Gospel. People responded in record numbers, so…we asked him to tour with our band.

The message Tony delivers is something that resonates with me. As he makes an appeal during Compassion presentations, he's not just preaching child sponsorship. He speaks about a merciful and gracious God, who could never love us more than He already does. God loves us because we are His—period. Hearing Tony talk inspires service and action, but not so God will love us more. Tony makes clear that our love for God and gratitude toward Him are the catalysts for our desire to serve, and that reaching out to others is truly the essence of Christianity.

When Tony told me he'd written a book, I was thrilled to hear more from him, more about his story and his relationship with a merciful God who loves us more than we can ever comprehend this side of heaven. *Serve One* is a truly moving collection of stories, quotes, and insights intended to motivate, convict, and guide us toward using our own unique gifts to serve others. I am proud to be beside Tony in his efforts for children living in extreme poverty, and I applaud this written endeavor as well. In it, there is humility, openness, and vulnerability. I appreciate Tony's willingness to talk about his own struggles. Even more, I am glad Tony Wolf is serving Jesus and asking others to do the same.

Bart Millard
Songwriter, Lead singer of MercyMe

If all we do is absent of Jesus, then this so-called love is completely in vain. —from "This So Called Love" by MercyMe

Introduction

Imagine if Jesus came to your house and ate with you tonight. What kind of dinner conversation would you have with Him?

I'm sure Jesus would show you mercy and help you. He'd heal any illnesses you had, inspire you with a creative story or two, and maybe even warn you about the false beliefs of phony religion.

If you're like me, you might be tempted to ask Him for answers to theological questions: "How does the Trinity work?" "Where exactly are heaven and hell?" "What were you doing all those years before your ministry in Galilee?" "When will the end of the world come?"

As you scoot your seat forward and lean in for profound answers to those big questions…Jesus does something you don't expect.

He changes the subject.

He asks about your finances and how much time you spend serving neighbors and when was the last time you almost went broke for the kingdom of God. Try as you might, there's no creating a diversion. Jesus won't let it go.

Then He gives you a startling command: "I want you to sell this house and everything in it. I want you to use all of your savings, empty out your 401k, cash in your stocks, move to a small village in Africa, and serve me in poverty for the rest of your life."

You burst out laughing, as if Jesus has just told a joke. Guffaw! "That's a good one, Jesus. Seriously, so when is the rapture?"

Jesus interrupts you again, saying, "I'm not

kidding. I'm asking you to forsake everything in your life, to uproot your family, go to a remote part of the world, and tell others the good news of the kingdom. And, by the way, no one will believe you, and the indigenous population will likely kill you for trying."

You are stunned. Utterly flummoxed. You feel the blood draining from your face. *How can Jesus ask me to do such a thing?* You think to yourself, *How can He demand this much from me*?

So here's the question: Would you answer the call? Or would you, like the rich young ruler of the Gospels, reject Jesus's command?

It's hard for those of us raised in Western culture to imagine a Savior who demands so much of us. It's difficult for us to fathom a God who would require such "sacrifice."

But Jesus hasn't asked this level of commitment from all of us. The Greeks to whom Paul first evangelized in the towns of Ephesus, Philippi, and Corinth lived out their days in the homes where they were raised, serving their communities, giving special offerings for missions, and being the light of the Gospels right in their neighborhoods.

Not everyone is called to be a missionary to Africa. But God has called all of us to support His work around the world and to live sacrificially for the kingdom of God.

In Matthew 6:24 (NIV), Jesus said to the hillside crowds in Galilee, "No one can serve two masters. Either you will hate the one and love the other, or you will be devoted to the one and despise the other. You cannot serve both God and money." The Savior spoke these words to some of the poorest people in the world. And it's no less true for us today.

We can't serve God *and* money.

But we can serve God *with* money.

In *Serve One*, author Tony Wolf challenges you to go beyond your comfort zone. To me, a comfort zone is an anxiety-neutral place where I am never challenged and can avoid unpleasant experiences. But Jesus means to shred the safe nests we've feathered and help us see that the harvest is plentiful, the workers are few, and the opportunity to love others is endless.

As you turn the pages of this short book, let the Spirit move you to choose a life of compassion. Our love for God is directly proportional to our capacity to serve those made in His image. Serving one master begins when we simply decide to serve one hurting, desperate soul at a time.

Dr. Jeff Kennedy
Author of *Father, Son, and the Other One: Experiencing the Holy Spirit as a Transforming, Empowering Reality*
Blogger at FearlessConversations.net

Getting Started

I once led worship at a camp in Tennessee. There, I met a young girl who was playing guitar. She sat on the floor with some chord diagrams, teaching herself choruses. As I listened, I was impressed by her singing. I asked, "Would you like to help me lead worship tomorrow night?"

She asked, "Me? You want me to help you?"

I said, "Why not?"

She lit up with excitement and hurried away to practice.

I walked away thinking, *Why did I do that? What if she freezes? What if she plays the wrong chords? What if it disrupts worship?* God had other ideas. As we facilitated worship that night, she was flawless. By the end of the night, I felt privileged to have played alongside her. It was a great night.

Years later I was at the Artist Appreciation Dinner for Compassion International. President Emeritus Wess Stafford spoke and talked about how singular moments can change our lives. After the dinner, a tall, confident college girl approached me. It was that same girl, Leslie, from Tennessee. "Tony, years ago you asked me to lead worship with you. I can't tell you what that meant to me. That was *my* moment." She went on to tell me that she was leading worship at a church in Franklin, Tennessee, and planned to make music her life. I didn't know why I asked her to help me all those years ago, but God did. God will use her to reach a ton of people I will never meet.

Paul wrote in 1 Corinthians 7:7, "Each of you has your own gift from God; one has this gift, another has that." We serve a God who slays giants through teenage boys. We serve a God whose Son conquered three days of death. What can he do with you? The answer is simple: whatever he wants and whatever you allow.

Moses was a man. The apostle Paul, Martin Luther King Jr., Billy Graham—each of these men submitted their lives to God. These men had one thing in common: They served. Sheepishly, one of my Bible college professors once told me, "If God can speak through Balaam's ass, then God can speak through you too." That might be a rough way of putting it, but it is true.

God moves through our abilities, but even more so through our availability. He penetrates hearts through the words of our mouths. He gives us thoughts that can revolutionize our world. He touches millions with a simple phrase. I've experienced it.

As a kid, I accompanied my youth minister to lead worship at a convention in Charlottesville, Virginia. The night before the convention, we were relaxing in our room when there was a knock. We opened the door to find a young guy with a guitar. He introduced himself and asked us if he could close out his concert with a worship song of his own. He said, "If you guys wouldn't mind, I'd like to close the concert with a song they can sing. Would you listen to the song and tell me what you think?"

We invited him in, and he sat down on the corner of a bed and sang a new chorus he'd recently written. He sang the chorus the next night at the convention. The man was Rich Mullins, and the song was "Awesome God." Over the years, with this simple chorus God moved millions to surrender their lives to Him.

When we serve, we can't begin to know what God will do with our acts of love. When we serve one person, that act may multiply and grow and spread far beyond our sight or knowledge. But certainly, if we don't serve, nothing will happen. It all begins when we serve. Even if it is writing one chorus like Rich did. Or inspiring one person, like Leslie.

My prayer is that this book serves as an encouragement to you. In Ephesians 3:20 (MSG) Paul says, "God can do anything, you know—far more than you could ever imagine or guess or request in your wildest dreams! He does it not by pushing us around but by working within us, his Spirit deeply and gently within us."

God is constantly moving, and He wants you to use the ability He has given you. He wants to impact others through your service, and you don't have to have a master's degree in theology to do it. Jesus's impact was made as a servant. With the same approach, we can experience life's greatest joy—serving others.

1

LIVE. LOVE. REPEAT.

What the world needs now is love, sweet love. It's the only thing that there's just too little of. What the world needs now is love, sweet love. No, not just for some but for everyone.
~ Hal David, lyricist

I have traveled the globe from Kenya to El Salvador to Ethiopia and back. In my travels I have seen many people existing in environments that seem to lack hope. I have spent time with children suffering, and even dying, from preventable diseases. I have looked into the faces of young people who did not know hope and were living desperate, destitute lives. Yet, in the midst of this carnage, I have also seen love.

In Narok, Kenya, I met a mother who gathered water each day for her little family. An otherwise routine and easy task was difficult and arduous for this mother of seven children. Three times a day she tied a towel, attached to a huge water jug, around her head and ran forty-five minutes one way to their water supply.

She braved the severe heat and wild animals each day, just to provide basic necessities for her kids. She told us of her encounters with elephants and rhinos and, once, a lioness. As she bent down to fill the water jug, she heard a sound and thought one of her children had followed her. She turned around, and the lion was within striking distance. Fortunately she was downwind from the beast, so it walked away. I asked what would've happened if she had been upwind from the lion and it picked up on her scent? Her arms moved in a quick, running motion, and she said, "I run very fast!" When an African woman runs among lions to fetch water for her children, that is love.

I met a single dad in El Salvador. He had four children, and just days after his youngest child was born, the mother took off and never came back. She even left her own mother there as well. So this young man literally worked three labor jobs and slept a few hours a night so his family could eat. Our tour guide explained, "This is a good man. He loves his family, but there are days when they don't eat. There are *weeks* when they don't eat. He is doing all he can." A young man laboring twenty hours a day for pennies on the hour so his family could survive—that is love.

We prayed for him, and as we were leaving, he grabbed my hand and talked. Our interpreter told me, "He wants you to promise that you will try to get help for the children of El Salvador."

I said, "I will." I turned to leave, and he grabbed me again, this time by the face.

He squeezed my cheeks like my grandmother used to on Christmas visits and said, in English, "No, you promise." I have been on this earth many years and never audibly heard the voice of God, but that was as close as I can imagine. With tears in his eyes, he gently spoke into my soul. So I did. I promised.

I knew I had to do something because, in some way, I could relate. When I was born, I was immediately placed into an orphanage in western Maryland. I was from a broken home before I even arrived. My biological father left when he found out I was on my way. By the time I was born, my biological mother had arranged for me to be taken in by the orphanage. I think my birth mom knew she was in way over her head. I'm sure she didn't *want* to give me up, but that is how it turned out. Being an orphan is not necessarily a great way for anyone to start life.

While this took place, another story was unfolding. A teenage girl decided she wanted to be a mother. She always had an overwhelming sense she was placed on Earth to be a mom. She wasn't focused on a career or college or anything else. She knew her place in the world was to be a mommy. Her husband-to-be was serving the US military in Vietnam at the time. Through their conversations and letters, she told him she wanted to be a mom, immediately. As soon as possible, naturally or through adoption—it didn't matter to her. She was supposed to be a mother.

That young GI wrote her letters, too, and encouraged her to look for a child who had no one else. They would take him or her in and raise that child as their very own. So she began to search. This search led her to me. Her young man returned from the war, and they were married. A short time later, they became my legal parents. They didn't know me and certainly didn't owe me anything. Two young people wanting to help the helpless—that is love.

In hindsight I now believe this was God's plan for me from the beginning. I know it was His plan for my mom as well. Mom and Dad always loved me unconditionally. They provided everything I needed, from the food I ate to the discipline every child needs. I was always told the truth about my adoption. I was always told I was special. I was told that so often that it cost my parents a little trip to see my school principal when I was in kindergarten. Seems I was telling the other kids something like, "I am special. My parents picked me out of hundreds of kids! Maybe thousands! Your parents were stuck with you!" Apparently, I even followed this up with some pointing and laughing. That night my dad taught me about humility, which made it hard for me to sit down for a little while.

Even in those moments of discipline, I was always told I was loved. I never had to wonder about that. My mom found out after adopting me that she was unable to give birth. She once told me, "I'm so glad that God laid the desire to be a mom on my heart so strongly when He did. Otherwise, even though I didn't know it then, I would have never been a mom." That woman has shown me love every day of my life from the first day I knew her. She was there for me when my birth family deserted me. That is love.

When it comes to love, talk is cheap. Everyone has within them what it takes to actually love others, and sometimes it takes just a little inspiration to find the courage and worthiness to act on that love. There are good people in this world willing to give, serve, and live out a life of real love and not just talk about it.

Jesus said in Matthew 7:21 (NIV), "Not everyone who says to me, 'Lord, Lord,' will enter the kingdom of heaven."

We are to live a life of love, according to Ephesians 5:2. Love requires action. Love is more than a trending topic or cool thing to be associated with. Love is not about our words. Love is manifested in our actions and through our service.

1 John 3:18 (NIV) says, "Dear children, let us not love with words or speech but with actions and in truth."

"Someday Someone is Going to Love Me Too"

In May 2010, while I was in El Salvador, I met a little girl who changed my life. We were on a home visit with two children sponsored through Compassion. When we arrived we found the two children but almost immediately discovered two other children were in the family as well. One was a little girl. She sat on the dirt floor of this tiny home. I remember ants being everywhere. When the girl saw the supplies and clean water we had brought, her face exploded into a wide, joyous smile. She talked to me at about eight hundred words a minute. I had no idea what she was saying. Other than the three or four words I've picked up from watching *Dora the Explorer* with my daughters, I know zero Spanish. I asked the interpreter what the little girl was saying. The interpreter told me she had said, "Someone in America loves my brother and sister, and someday someone is going to love me too."

It broke my heart. I know what it's like to feel unwanted or unloved. I also know what happens when we pour love into the life of a child who perceives none. After meeting her—and accepting the challenge of that El Salvadoran father who made me promise I would help—I came home and called Compassion International. I thought it would be great if I could help connect 365 children with a sponsor in one year. I thought if I could help one child a day for a year, that would be wonderful! God had another goal in mind. In the following three years, I would see over fifteen thousand children get sponsored in my travels.

I have been to many small towns where employment is scarce, congregations living with little to get by on, much less to give. I preached in a small country church last fall. That Sunday morning attendance, including infants, was twenty-nine. I shared my personal story, and talked about the people I had met in El Salvador and Kenya, and asked each person to consider sponsoring a child. Then, something beautiful happened. Every person in that building walked back to the table. One couple told me they were out of work but decided to sponsor two children. A teenager came by and said he could mow lawns to earn money and wanted to sponsor a child. Another family asked for a stack of child packets to look through. I handed them ten packets. The family sponsored all ten. Twenty minutes later, seventeen children had been released from poverty…by a church of twenty-nine people. That is love.

I recently spoke at a Catalyst West conference at Mariners Church in California. While I was there, I heard Bryan Loritts, a pastor from Memphis, say, "If you claim to be a Christian and do nothing for those in need, there is no proof you are changed. If you do not engage the poor, you will not inherit the kingdom of God."

We are called to serve. These orders come straight from the One who sent His only child into this world as an example to us, for all of mankind. Jesus's impact was made through service and love. That is the example of our Lord. And that is Christianity. You live. You love. And you do it all over again.

2

BECOMING A DIVA

I'd love to be a diva. But then I'd have to send so many apology notes for my abhorrent behavior.
~ Amy Adams

Some people liken being adopted to being the last kid picked in kick ball.

I never did.

For me, it was much more like the story of Moses. Thanks to my adoptive parents, a childhood in Pharaoh's palace couldn't have been much better. Growing up on the income of a blue-collar book printer, I never had my own chariot or chest of gold like Moses. I did have a '77 Ford Maverick, a ton of Beatles vinyls, and what seemed like the world in the palm of my hand—that's right, I had an Atari. Now, years of video pong can be blamed every time I draw a blank, forget something important, or daydream myself into a drool.

Despite my materialistically humble beginnings, I look back now appreciating the plan God had for my life. Regardless of where we are or what we're doing, God has a plan for us all. I truly understand Psalms 139:13–16 (NASB):

> For You formed my inward parts;
> You wove me in my mother's womb.
> I will give thanks to You, for I am fearfully and wonderfully made;

> Wonderful are Your works,
> And my soul knows it very well.
> My frame was not hidden from You,
> When I was made in secret,
> And skillfully wrought in the depths of the earth;
> Your eyes have seen my unformed substance;
> And in Your book were all written
> The days that were ordained for me,
> When as yet there was not one of them.

My first church-based experiences were Vacation Bible School, youth camp, and activities at a small church on the Mason-Dixon Line. My parents demonstrated the character of Christ when they took me in. That said, we weren't in church every single Sunday. Sometimes Dad would hear about a fried-chicken dinner at church and say, "Get in the truck. They're having chicken at church, and we're going!" Mom loved when some Southern gospel group came to perform a concert. My friends and I loved these groups because they all had that one guy who sang amazingly low and ridiculously loud. The crazy loud bass guy always broke off some phrase six octaves below everyone else. And, yes, we were laughing at them, not with them.

When I was fifteen, I wanted to go every Sunday because I knew Marcy, the prettiest girl I'd ever seen, would be there. Between cantatas, chili cook-offs, and the occasional ministerial firings, hirings, and resignations under mysterious circumstances, we all had our motives for wanting to be there on any given Sunday.

I was working at McDonald's one Sunday night when a friend from church came into the restaurant to talk to me. Sean and I had hit it off at an early age because we both did impersonations. As a kid, I was a big fan of legendary impersonator Rich Little. After seeing him perform, I began entering school talent shows, doing my best impressions of Porky Pig, Muhammad Ali, and Darth Vader. I brought my show to Sunday school as well. Sean always chimed right in with his imitations of David Lee Roth, Howard Cosell, or Woody Woodpecker. Our Sunday school teacher was an older woman named Mrs. Palmer, one of the sweetest ladies I've ever met. While she tried to direct the class to the Gospel of Luke, we would belt out our depiction of Popeye meeting Barney Rubble. Mrs. Palmer must have danced a naked jig when we graduated her class.

Sean told me about a concert he'd seen at church. "They were funny, and they rocked. This band was awesome!" Sean said. He went on to tell me that this group, called Son's Up, was planning to take forty teenagers on tour to perform a musical. I wasn't big on musicals…or my being in them. Sean told me, "They need a rhythm guitar player, so I told them about you." I had been teaching myself guitar. This was before the unwritten law that now requires every youth leader to learn guitar.

As a teen, I remembered John Lennon's tragic murder. I was impressed with the effect Lennon and the Beatles had on people. I saw the footage of fans screaming, people passing out, and thousands of girls crying. Girls were all the motivation I needed to play guitar. I learned "Stairway To Heaven" and "Sweet

Home Alabama," and quickly began entertaining friends. My friend Mike Shafer and I performed "Norwegian Wood" at our high school's annual pop concert. There were tuning issues, timing issues, and "somebody should've loved us enough to stop us" issues. Despite all of these issues, that night gave me confidence.

So I called Jay Banks, the lead singer and founder of Son's Up, at tiny Roanoke Bible College (since renamed Mid-Atlantic Christian University, or MACU) in Elizabeth City, North Carolina. By "tiny" I mean two hundred students, no football team, and a handful of graduates each year. Shortly after my call, I received a letter of acceptance as a member of the musical production. Jay wrote songs and skits, and was a natural at connecting with people. Jay was an encourager. He could convince an Oompa Loompa that he could play basketball for the University of North Carolina. On the tour, I saw many lives changed in the audience, as well as onstage.

For the next two years, I served as Jay's protégé in youth ministry in Cary, North Carolina, and as a member of Son's Up. We wrote music together, played basketball a lot, and led worship at national conventions. Jay told me I should consider going to Bible college. No one in my family tree had ever gone to college. Jay might as well have said, "You should try out for the Yankees." Me, go to college? I barely made it through high school. Regardless of my apprehensions, a few months later, with forty-eight dollars to my name, I was a college freshman.

I never planned to go to college, so I never took the SAT or ACT college admission exams.

Fortunately, Roanoke Bible College (RBC) did not require an SAT from me. Based on the assortment of fruitcakes and carnies who surrounded me at freshman orientation, the ability to *spell* SAT might not have been a requirement. The class included a Lucky the Leprechaun look-alike, a bearded lady, a guy who ate pizza with his toes, a seventy-two-year-old woman, and a bear. Oh, sure, he convinced the financial aids people that he was a Viking, but I knew all along he was a bear. Standing in the middle of the freak show I thought, *I can't believe it. I'm paying thousands of dollars to be in the circus.*

My freshman year was rough. My grades were just good enough to keep me in school, while the old woman made the dean's list and the bear did surprisingly well. I was more concerned about people knowing I wrote my own music than conveying any essential message during performances. I also passed on dating some very godly young women because I was infatuated with physical appearances and insecure about myself. I was shallow and immature.

One of my most important pieces of advice to you as you read this book is to learn contentment. Paul wrote to his friends in Philippi, in Philippians 4:11–12 (NIV), "I have learned to be content whatever the circumstances. I know what it is to be in need, and I know what it is to have plenty. I have learned the secret of being content in any and every situation." Seek out the value and opportunities of each day. This day, this time, these breaths are yours only because God is giving them to you.

I wasted many precious chances to love others because I looked at those opportunities as steppingstones rather than immediate gifts. Writer Robert Brault once said, "Enjoy the little things in life, for one day you will look back and realize that they were the big things." Sadly, my life was dominated by discontent.

Paul wrote this to Timothy in 1 Timothy 6:6–12 (NASB):

> But godliness actually is a means of great gain when accompanied by contentment. For we have brought nothing into the world, so we cannot take anything out of it either. If we have food and covering, with these we shall be content. But those who want to get rich fall into temptation and a snare and many foolish and harmful desires which plunge men into ruin and destruction. For the love of money is a root of all sorts of evil, and some by longing for it have wandered away from the faith and pierced themselves with many griefs.
>
> But flee from these things, you man of God, and pursue righteousness, godliness, faith, love, perseverance and gentleness. Fight the good fight of faith; take hold of the eternal life to which you were called, and you made the good confession in the presence of many witnesses.

Righteousness and godliness were qualities I had only read about. It took time for me to learn that "making it" was all about losing it. People aren't touched by our academic degrees or accolades, but through the depth of our character and love for people.

RBC's groundskeeper, a man named Phil Alligood, was from eastern North Carolina. Alligood, as we all called him, was a loud and energetic man—essential qualities for anyone who pushes a lawn mower twenty-one hours a day. He was also responsible for building maintenance and repairs. He called me aside one day after chapel. "You see that window over there?" he asked. He pointed to a window I had broken the night before. RBC had numerous piano practice rooms in the main building. I practiced piano in those rooms almost every night. Some nights, however, the building was locked early. Having little regard for any rules I might fracture, I bypassed the locked doors by climbing through a cafeteria window. This time, I put a hole in the screen and had bent it. Knowing somehow that I was the culprit, Alligood glared at me and said, "Tony, I'm concerned for you. The little things define who you are. And the little things could be your downfall."

I felt hurt, thinking he saw me as a bad apple. I thought he said what he'd said because he didn't like me. Later I reasoned, *What if Mr. Alligood cares?* Maybe he felt I was worth his time. Maybe he pried himself from his tractor because he saw potential. Over the next few years, though Alligood and I never exchanged Christmas cards or anything, I came to know him as a man of honesty and integrity. He made his biggest impact by simply being real and saying what needed to be said. He probably didn't even realize he was making an impression. That's how most people who make a difference operate. Their impact is a by-product of who they are and how they love.

In 1 Timothy 4:11 (MSG), Paul tells Timothy,

"And don't let anyone put you down because you're young. Teach believers with your life: by word, by demeanor, by love, by faith, by integrity." The example I was setting was not one of integrity. I was dishonest, aloof, and undisciplined. I was a self-absorbed diva. After a few more juvenile blunders similar to the window caper, our RBC President Bill Griffin advised me to start over at another school. It was right about then that I began to realize I had a lot of growing up to do.

Author C.S. Lewis once wrote, "True humility is not thinking less of yourself; it is thinking of yourself less." Divas are too worried about themselves to even think about another person, much less serve one. We realize our true potentials and live with real purpose when we stop being completely focused on and engrossed in ourselves. Humility paves the road to a world of people we can serve. I had to simply look past myself.

3

WAREHOUSE HUMILITY

It was pride that changed angels into devils; it is humility that makes men as angels.
~ Saint Augustine

Something I realize increasingly as I mature is that God seems to teach us the most when we appear to have the least. I went home to Maryland that first summer after Bible college and worked as a forklift operator for a company called Wetterau, a grocery and produce distributor. As an operator, I was responsible for pulling store orders, picking the pieces, loading them onto a skid, and delivering them to the docks. Easy, except for a few minor details.

First, there was "the physical"—never see a doctor who has the words *Louisville Slugger* etched onto one of his fingers. Second, I worked the graveyard shift…in the freezer. Finally, warehouses are not for you if you aren't in shape. If I were to work there today, I'd probably wind up in the intensive care unit in critical condition. We were required to load three hundred pieces an hour—that's five items per minute. If, in the course of a weeklong period, you averaged 299 pieces or less, you lost your job. Routine necessities, like going to the bathroom, became calculated risks for fear of getting behind.

One night, while lifting water jugs out of a bottom bin, I felt something I hope to never feel again. A torn groin muscle is a most painful thing that takes place in a most delicate area. I went straight down onto the cold, grimy concrete. As I rolled onto my back, I remember thinking, *Do you know why you are lying here, holding your privates, rolling around on a frozen warehouse floor at 4:30 in the morning?* I knew the answer. I was there for the same reason Peter fell under the waters as he walked toward Jesus on the sea: I wasn't focused on Jesus. I had lost sight of what was critical, and it happened gradually, largely because of my irresponsibility with the little things. Alligood was right. That broken window at RBC was only a symptom of a more serious illness.

When I was a young boy, my father always said, "It's not the things you do that get you in trouble; it's the things that you don't do that get you in trouble." That was true when I was a kid and still valid as a young man. I was irresponsible with new jackets, lunch money, and homework as a kid, and equally negligent with my spirituality as an adult.

As is always the case, God knew what was best for me. I wasn't supposed to be on a lighted stage, leading hundreds of people. I was instead learning his will in a dark and sullied warehouse. As I lay on the floor in burning-groin agony, I thought to myself, *I am never going to be in this position again. I will serve where God puts me, when God sends me with what God has given me.* I was off work for a week or so to heal, but the reality of my position was that I had two more months in the warehouse. I wasn't exactly thrilled but, thankfully, God had a plan.

Based on the cast of characters I worked with that summer, the warehouse looked more like Arkham Asylum than a workplace. Jim was a Shaggy look-alike, who rode his lift at high speeds while doing loud Popeye impersonations. Another guy, also named Tony, could pick 540 pieces an hour while the rest of our crew averaged around 360. Company officials knew Tony was pumping himself full of "junk," but having a guy who could pick twice as fast as anyone else proved invaluable to them (guess who mysteriously always got around company drug tests). I worked with ex-convicts, mentally unstable individuals, and drug addicts. Then there were John and Rob.

John was a rare talent capable of using his favorite curse word eight times in one sentence. He'd use it as a noun, a verb, an adjective and, of course, an interjection. He was a nice guy otherwise, but was not seeking a spiritual lifestyle (or vocabulary for that matter). One night, John and I were the only two operators on the floor. The trucks were running late, so we waited in the break room for the onslaught of orders to come. John asked me a ton of questions about my faith. He knew very little about the Bible or Jesus. In the weeks to come, we had several more conversations, and one day before work, John asked, "How can I become a Christian?" We sat down and talked, and before I knew what was going on, John asked me to baptize him. We talked a couple more times, he got his girlfriend and some family together, and we went to a local church one morning after work and I baptized him. God was using me…and he wasn't finished.

Rob had been my best friend growing up. We traded video games, listened to Run DMC, and played sandlot football together almost every weekend. Rob became increasingly curious about what it meant to be a Christian, especially after I trained for the ministry. Rob needed a job a few weeks after I started at Wetterau, so I told my supervisor and Rob's application managed to make its way to the top of the heap. Rob called to tell me how excited he was about getting the job. I did *not*, however, tell him about "the physical."

Rob and I spent a lot of time together that summer, and after numerous discussions and a couple of Bible studies, Rob was ready to take the plunge too. It was a special day for me because Rob and I were more like brothers than friends. Rob was family to me. God was moving in my life like never before, and as a result, my best friend and an unlikely coworker had decided to follow Jesus. I had left my spiritual college surroundings feeling broken, and got fixed in a warehouse where broken spirits surrounded me.

I decided that fall to return to RBC, despite the advice of President Griffin. I felt I had let certain people down, casting an unsavory image on them by their association with me. I wanted to do well, to vindicate myself as well as the people who believed in me. Of course, these weren't correct motives. One day at lunch, I explained my ambitions to a mentor, a graduate minister named Tony Krantz. Tony said, "You could never please everyone all the time, even if you were perfect. Just look how it went for Jesus. Just make sure that love is the motivation behind everything you do and you'll be fine." Tony is the best piano player I've ever met and a good songwriter, and I looked up to him for that. Tony was an incredibly bright man, who gave me incalculable advice and encouragement. The benefit of others, which is *all* of humanity, should be our goal in anything we attempt.

One Son's Up song simply says, "Less of me and more of you." After my encounters with people like Mr. Alligood and President Griffin, a summer at the warehouse, and some serious personal reevaluation, it was clear something had to change. With the "less of me" mentality, I tried a different approach.

Garrett Lewis convinced me that RBC was where I needed to be. "Pop" was the dean of students and head coach of our basketball team. He was also in charge of special events on campus. Pop had one arm withered by polio when he was an infant, yet he still played basketball with us. One time a player challenged Pop to a free-throw contest. My teammate made fifteen in a row. Pop stepped to the line and sank sixty-seven consecutive free throws. One night during my junior season, Pop was frustrated with the officiating. We were leading big late in the game, and I was sitting beside him on the bench. He sighed heavily, waved his hand, and said "Tony, get back in there and do something!"

I asked him, "Who do you want me to go in for?"

He said, "Just walk out there."

I said, "Pop, it'll be six-on-five."

Pop grinned, "They haven't noticed anything else tonight; they won't notice you either." I played for a minute and a half, scoring four points before they noticed and called a technical foul on me. I love Pop.

I asked Pop if I could be part of a recruitment effort called "High School Days." He asked what I had in mind, and I told him about my summer. I wanted to impact prospective students who would be at this event, but I also wanted to inspire my classmates to do the same. As I looked around campus, it looked a lot like Wetterau to me. Many people just needed a nudge in the right direction for God to really work on them and through them. I looked to cast people who'd never had an opportunity in this arena: a forty-member cast of people who had never sung, acted, or worked a production before. Forty people with the "less of me" mentality.

Mother Teresa once said, "Give yourself fully to God. He will use you to accomplish great things on the condition that you believe much more in His love than in your own weakness." At worst, I felt a united labor of love by our student body would result in benefit for Christ. When a group makes a statement, it lessens the role of the individual. That's one of the many beautiful things about the concept of "church." While I organized the effort, our students ultimately facilitated the ministry that was to take place. I hoped it would be like the Son's Up tours I had been a part of, lives changed in the audience and onstage. Pop agreed to give it a chance.

I was twenty-three years old and, for the first time, had completely turned everything over to God. Again, most of these cast members weren't great singers, spectacular actors, or amazingly talented people; they were simply willing. Most already had the "less of me" mind-set. God desires acts of love from us, not performances. 1 Peter 5:5–7 (NASB) says, "You younger men, likewise, be subject to your elders; and all of you, clothe yourselves with humility toward one another, for God is opposed to the proud, but gives grace to the humble. Therefore humble yourselves under the mighty hand of God, that He may exalt you at the proper time, casting all your anxiety on Him, because He cares for you."

He does care for you. His Son took the world by love, not by force. Jesus Christ wasn't a superstar; he was a servant, modeling greatness through service for us. In John 13:5–17 (NASB), Jesus is with His disciples:

> Then He poured water into the basin, and began to wash the disciples' feet and to wipe them with the towel with which He was girded. So He came to Simon Peter. He said to Him, "Lord, do You wash my feet?" Jesus answered and said to him, "What I do you do not realize now, but you will understand hereafter." Peter said to Him, "Never shall You wash my feet!" Jesus answered him, "If I do not wash you, you have no part with Me." Simon Peter said to Him, "Lord, then wash not only my feet, but also my hands and my head." Jesus said to him, "He who has bathed needs only to wash his feet, but is completely clean; and you are clean, but not all of you." For He knew the one who was betraying Him; for this reason He said, "Not all of you are clean."'
>
> So when He had washed their feet, and taken His garments and reclined at the table again, He said to them, "Do you know what I have done to you? You call Me Teacher and Lord; and you are right, for so I am. If I then, the

> Lord and the Teacher, washed your feet, you also ought to wash one another's feet. For I gave you an example that you also should do as I did to you. Truly, truly, I say to you, a slave is not greater than his master, nor is one who is sent greater than the one who sent him. If you know these things, you are blessed if you do them."

In the face of betrayal and the knowledge of his impending crucifixion, Christ found it most important to model service. Jesus shows His disciples that there is blessing in serving and through helping others.

The night of our High School Days production was incredible. God moved numerous people to come forward, and many decisions were made in the audience and onstage. I saw people serving one another. I saw love. While all of this went on around me, I remembered lying on the dirty warehouse floors of Wetterau and was grateful that even at my dirtiest, in my most broken and cynical moments, God still wanted to use me. Humility learned in a warehouse taught me that the world is only better when we serve people one at a time. We must humbly serve others the way Jesus served us.

4

RICK LOOKS LIKE JESUS

A life of enthusiasm, hope, and contributions through one's own gifts is a life well lived.
~ Unknown

Roanoke Bible College was a great place for me. The five years I spent on the Outer Banks were invaluable. The monetary price of education, even back then, was high. I realize that every month when I get my bill from the College Loan Foundation. At times, as I write out that check, I think, *Was it worth it?* However, I have come to realize, as my adult life teaches me, the cost of ignorance is momentous. I am grateful for my college education, but life experiences continue to be my greatest educator. The sad thing is, I left college uneducated in some fundamental areas of my life. And I wasn't the only one.

I remember something a minister once said to me years earlier. Before my friend Jay talked me into going to college, I worked every odd job imaginable. I had been a paperboy in junior high, flipped burgers in high school for three years, delivered pizzas, worked construction, sold shoes, and worked as a surveyor for the US Geological Survey. During my time with the Survey, I was attacked by locusts, found myself searching for anacondas (yes, in North Carolina), and took a screwdriver to the hand (it had to be removed by a coworker in the field). Being a surveyor was a monotonous toil, spent oftentimes in a full bodysuit or waders in the summer heat.

I left the field early one day and stopped in to the church to see Jay but was greeted by the lead pastor. He was a highly educated man with more degrees than a right angle. He was generally a nice guy but never seemed to look kindly on the "uneducated." I stood covered in sweat, with mud all over my pants and boots, asking where Jay was. He told me Jay was visiting someone at the hospital. Then, noting it was only early afternoon, he said, "Shouldn't you be working?"

Jokingly and in light of the extreme heat on this day, I said, "That's easy for you to say, sitting in the AC and eating your lunch behind that desk." Sarcastic humor is the most dangerous form of humor there is. His demeanor totally changed.

With a scowl, he said to me, "I have a master's degree son. I've earned the right to sit behind a desk." Then he shut the door, which of course, then locked.

I didn't feel much love in his attitude that day. As Christians, the rights we have earned are best summarized in Ephesians 2:4–9 (NASB):

> But God, being rich in mercy, because of His great love with which He loved us, even when we were dead in our transgressions, made us alive together with Christ (by grace you have been saved), and raised us up with Him, and seated us with Him in the heavenly places in Christ Jesus, so that in the ages to come He might show the surpassing riches of His grace in kindness toward us in Christ Jesus. For by grace you have been saved through faith; and that not of yourselves, it is the gift of God; not

as a result of works, so that no one may boast.

The grace that saves us is the free, undeserved goodness of God, and he saves not because of our achievements, academic degrees, or trophies, but by his grace. It is beautiful when you witness someone discovering this truth.

I once attended a youth camp near Pittsburgh and met a young lady who was confused. She had planned to go to a Christian college and enter into full-time Christian service. Her church, however, approached her and told her their children's pastor was leaving and that they were interested in hiring her to fill his position. She told me, "I don't know what to do. I don't have any training, and I feel that I need an education in order to do an adequate job." She told me this just after praying for and hugging on kids from her church; the students had just come forward for prayer following a challenging and inspiring message.

"You don't need a degree to do what you just did," I said. "There are no degrees in caring. There are no classes on empathy, comforting the crying, or on God-given rapport." She hugged me and scampered off to find her group.

College was a great place for me. I learned much. I had time to grow up there too. It was a place that taught me many life lessons. Years later, long after college, it has become clear to me that our genuine love for others is more important than all the knowledge and credentials we can compile. Our willingness to serve those in need far exceeds our academic accomplishments. I went to school with many people who had high GPA's and never understood that. They never really "got it." Fortunately, God has used me through my own immaturity and ignorance. I still learn through my many challenges, setbacks, and humbling experiences in my life.

One of my best friends in the world is my old college pal Rick Robie. Rick wasn't your typical Bible college student. Rick loved Van Halen, had big hair, and loved to laugh. Rick was always bucking the system and getting into trouble with the staff. Rick played jokes on people and games like "spray the guy in the bathroom stall with the fire hose" and "pee in the tea"—don't ask. Rick spent most of his senior year serving a punishment for leaving the dorm after curfew to get pancakes. He wasn't getting beer, hooking up with chicks, or engaging in something criminal; he just wanted pancakes. He should have been excommunicated.

Rick's grades put him in the middle of the pack when we graduated. As for me, if it weren't for my good friend Davon, I would've been the dumbest person in my class. Seriously, I am sure I graduated second from last. Again, RBC was a small school so it's always nice to tell people I graduated twenty-fifth in my class. I just never tell them there were only twenty-six of us who walked the stage at graduation.

Rick has been serving people ever since. He has a natural rapport with everyone he meets. He's fun to be around, and kids love him. Simply put, Rick looks like Jesus by his actions. A while ago, we received news that a couple of our classmates had committed criminal offenses while serving as ministers and teachers. Despite being academically sound and good friends to me, these guys did prison time. Compared to a humble heart, love, and availability, education is worthless in the arena of service. The best-case scenario is when a person combines the things cerebrally learned with a selfless heart and lots of love.

Let me be perfectly clear. Some of the biggest difference makers I have met in this world greatly benefited from their college educations. The accomplishments of their college years were products of much hard work. Oftentimes their degrees resulted in many opened doors to minister to and serve the masses, which otherwise might have been closed.

That said, my admiration for people has little to do with the paper certificates that hang on their office walls. I admire the father of four who works overtime so his daughters can take a dance class. That is love. I respect the people who give up their Saturday night bowling league to clean the church building the night before service. There are people who could be making a generous living here in America and, instead, live in financial poverty in West Africa to pursue wild souls with the message of Jesus. That is love.

Some of the best examples of Christian service and generosity I know are guys with doctorates, and some of the best examples of Christian service and generosity I know are people who barely earned a high-school diploma. The real issue is this: Degrees or none, are you committed to serving and looking like Jesus?

5

IS IT IN YOU?

After all you've done for me, I've responded selfishly. Here I am, so ashamed, tell me what to do. Try me now, show me how. Can I be used some way, somehow? All I ask is make my life count for you.

~ Jay Banks, from the song
"Make My Life Count"

I really liked *Saving Private Ryan.* In the movie, Tom Hanks stars as Captain John Miller, who leads a small group of soldiers into hostile territory on a mission to rescue young soldier Private James Ryan. Private Ryan's three other brothers die, almost simultaneously, in World War II. The soldiers in Captain Miller's group fall one by one during this rescue until only a couple of soldiers are left to protect Private Ryan. In a closing scene, Captain Miller is gunned down just as Private Ryan reaches safety. As he sits on a bridge dying, Captain Miller pulls Ryan close and says, "Earn this. Earn it." In essence, Captain Miller was saying, "Several of us died saving you. Make your life count."

Jesus laid down his life. He entered a hostile environment, and His mission was to save us. He died and resurrected to show us we could reach safety. We could never earn or repay His sacrifice—we didn't deserve it. However, at the very least, our gratitude should drive us to honor Him. What can we do in response to grace? We can respond to it by giving of ourselves through love. Because we are so deeply loved, we love in return. Paul's thought was, *Let us live up to what we have already attained.* We should be willing, at the very least, to serve. Live a life of service as an act of appreciation.

The idea of serving isn't a popular one in our society. We exalt home-run hitters while dismissing the guy who lays down the bunt. We want ripped abs from a seven-minute, twice-a-month workout. We expect to win wars without the first casualty. Courage is not always glamorous. Rare is the man who lays down his life in this world for the cause of others. It was inspiring to see firefighters rush into the flaming, crumbling towers of the World Trade Center during one of the worst tragedies in our nation's history. Those heroic men and women were more concerned about the people still inside the towers than in their own well-being.

Jesus said in John 15:13 (NASB), "Greater love has no one than this, that one lay down his life for his friends." He later proved his belief in that statement by going to Calvary to erase the sins of the world. Jesus understood, preached, and modeled service and sacrifice. Jesus didn't just talk about service—He lived it.

When my wife and I moved to Nashville in 2002, we only knew a couple of guys I had recorded music with the year before. One of those guys, Peter Vaque, modeled the true meaning of service almost immediately after we arrived in Music City. Knowing I was starting a new ministry, Peter offered me part-time work with his company installing lighting and sound systems. My first week, I agreed to drive to Tampa to help him with a church install. We took turns driving, and I happened to be behind the wheel at 4:30 a.m. as we crossed the Florida state line and came upon a terrible accident.

In the middle of Interstate 75, a boat had come off its hitch and flipped. People were running in the middle of the road, cars were running off the road—it was chaotic. Somehow I maneuvered Peter's van through the many obstacles and off to the side of an exit ramp. During the next hour, Peter showed me a level of service and heroism many people never have the privilege of witnessing in a lifetime.

Peter jumped out of the van, directing me to his first-aid kit and towels as he grabbed flashlights and bottled water. Seconds later, I was sprinting down the ramp with an armful of supplies, trying to keep up with Peter. He jumped over the guardrail and made his way toward a van that had rolled in the accident. As I approached the van, I saw about forty people standing there, seemingly frozen in place. Peter quickly helped a little girl and her mother climb out of the top of the van. The mother was in shock. Tiny spots of blood splattered on her face, she talked about Disney World and the weather and what time they would arrive at the park. I handed them each a towel and turned my attention back to the van. Peter was now on top of the van, shining his flashlight down inside. The father was inside, pinned by a seat. When Peter realized the father was OK, he asked, "Is everyone else out?"

The father responded, "My boy is in the back."

Peter jumped down off the van and hurried to the back as I followed. When he opened the door, I immediately knew something was terribly wrong. Peter looked onto the side of the road and yelled, "Is anyone here medically trained?"

Two women raised their hands, each saying, "I'm a nurse."

Peter implored them, "I need your help!" He told me to lay a couple of towels down on the highway as he reached for the motionless body of a young boy. Apparently, he had fallen asleep on a bed in the back of the van and wasn't wearing a seat belt. When the van rolled, the rear glass busted. As the van slid on its side, the boy dragged on the pavement. He was suffering from massive head trauma and bleeding profusely. Peter told the nurses, "We have to move his head to the side; he's choking." They proceeded to tilt his head to the side. Just then, a car came flying through the accident scene, almost hitting Peter and one of the nurses.

Helicopters and rescue units converged on the scene. I asked a paramedic if there was any chance the boy might live. Before I could even finish my question, she closed her eyes and shook her head, "No." Peter continued to hold the boy's hand, wiping his face until medics loaded him onto a stretcher. Then, with a face full of tears, Peter joined me on the side of the road. For a minute as I looked up at Peter, I forgot the accident and all that was happening around me. I was in awe. From the second we stopped our van, Peter turned away all concern for his own apprehensions, legal implications, and personal safety to turn his focus on serving a family he had never even seen before. Peter proved to be, in the most adverse situation, a servant of men.

Theologian Albert Schweitzer once wisely stated, "I don't know what your destiny will be, but one thing I know: The ones among you who will be really happy are those who have sought and found how to serve." During my tenure in the Tampa area, I met a man named Charles. Charles was a tall, somewhat intimidating, white-haired gentleman who proved to be just that. He was a soft-spoken, pleasant, and gentle man. He loved traditional hymns but appreciated the modern worship that was "winning the young families" at our youthful congregation. He was a good family man and time-honored Christian soldier in my eyes.

One day after service, Charles stood and announced his doctors had told him he had cancer and very little time left on this earth. The announcement came as a shock to most, and not long after that Charles began to fade fast. When his hospice care ended, he and his wife requested that members of the church help provide care in his final days. Having never watched a man die before, I was a bit apprehensive. During three eight-hour shifts that week, I learned this: There is no greater call than to serve someone in need.

Charles was about six-foot-three, and although his weight dropped in the final weeks, Charles was heavy. During my second shift, he had to go to the bathroom. He could hardly speak, but he managed to whisper and point in a manner that I understood. I slowly helped him get sideways on the bed. He was sweating profusely. As I attempted to lift him, I caught a glimpse of him looking at me. He seemed humiliated. I recognized the shame he must have been feeling, having his church's youth minister lift him out of bed to use the bathroom. I have never felt a greater sense of compassion in my life. I pulled his neck close to mine and hugged him. The words that came next were not scholarly but from my heart. "It's cool, Charles, you know…it's all right," I said as he squeezed my neck and cried. To this day, I have never known a more genuine and honest emotion.

Mother Teresa told us that God comes to us through suffering human beings. Recent studies suggest the benefits of serving others extend far beyond what we might expect. Research suggests serving others can actually have a positive physical impact on your health. They call it "the helper's high," and it might even be beneficial to the immune system. A University of Michigan study showed life expectancy increases for people who volunteer. A study of elderly Japanese found those who provide assistance to others rated their health more favorably compared with older adults less involved in their communities. Studies at Yale, Johns Hopkins, University of California, National Institute of Mental Health, and Ohio State support similar findings.

We all possess a deep need to make a difference in the lives of others, and serving teaches us that our lives have meaning. Maya Angelou said, "If you find it in your heart to care for somebody else, you will have succeeded." Nothing could be truer.

What is in your heart? You might not really know until you are in *that* moment…

That moment when you drive up on an accident.

That moment when you are at the bedside of a dying friend.

That moment when one person *needs* your

help.

Loving others can be a natural impulse. Helping those in need just seems to be a sensible reaction in moments of distress. Serving can also be uncomfortable at times. Service often requires us to leave our warm, cozy, and protected environments. But service always leads to greater satisfaction in life and a greater impact for God's kingdom. We simply have to look within, where the Spirit enables us to be more like Him. Is it in you?

6

KATRINA

God gave you a gift of 86,400 seconds today. Have you used even one to say "thank you"?
~ William Ward, missionary

After Hurricane Katrina devastated the southeast, I had an opportunity to help with the cleanup effort in Pass Christian, Mississippi, with Campus Crusade for Christ. Our church sent all of our members an e-mail asking for volunteers. My wife, Laura, and I prayed about it and decided I should go. We called, they were delighted, and then they sent us some information and waivers to sign. Call me crazy, but I usually become nervous when I see words like "hepatitis," "disease," "accident," and "death." I tend to get concerned when reading phrases like "exposure to dead persons," "toxic environmental conditions," and "emotionally disturbing conditions or persons." What if something bad were to happen to me? What if I were to bring back some type of disease? What if I didn't come back?

After considering the issue at hand, we believed I should still go on the trip. A few days earlier, as I watched the coverage of New Orleans, I said to Laura, "I wish I could help." God answers prayer and, sometimes, wishes too. We filled out the paperwork, signed the "death papers," and Laura packed my things. The e-mails they sent us said I would be helping to cut down trees, digging mud out of people's homes, and moving damaged furniture. I know as much about chainsaws and tractors as Al Gore knows about inventing the Internet, and despite my athletic background, when it comes to brute strength, I am more like Olive Oyl than Popeye.

I was to ride down with the guy who was transporting a tractor. He pulled up to the church office in an old, beat-up pickup truck that looked like it had seen its share of wars. Tobacco juice and spit was splattered all over the dashboard. He introduced himself with a firm handshake. Rob looked like the guy who played high-school football and belonged to Future Farmers of America. He said, "I hope speed doesn't make you nervous, because I drive like a maniac." I laughed and told him I didn't mind a bit. In truth I didn't know Rob, and I was nervous.

During the long drive, I got to know Rob. He was actually a nurse, which immediately made me feel a little better about any injuries I might suffer. He worked in a hospital operating room and had several stories about what happens when things go wrong. We talked about his job for a couple of hours, and I was fascinated. From his stories and willingness to be on the trip, I knew he was a person who genuinely wanted to help others.

As we approached Gulfport, Mississippi, we noticed trees down on both sides of the highway. Also downed were highway signs, a mangled golden arch over a McDonald's, and smashed or completely missing hotel and restaurant signs. We saw military vehicles on the beach. We didn't see damaged houses as much as we saw flattened lots. There were crushed vehicles and other debris, like refrigerators, computers, and televisions. One pile of rubble bore a small Waffle House sign that read, "We will rebuild."

Eventually we stopped at a military checkpoint. We told them we were going to Pass Christian, and the guard said, "Oh, it's really bad there."

I thought, *What could be worse than complete annihilation?*

We took detours and side streets toward our destination. Along the way, we saw guys sitting in lawn chairs and holding shotguns in front of their properties. Spray-painted signs read, "You Loot, We Shoot," "Go Ahead, Make My Day," and "You'll Never Take Me Alive." I had never seen anything like it. We arrived in Pass Christian, located our camp, and set up tents outside Trinity Episcopal Church. This once-beautiful structure had been gutted by a forty-two-foot storm surge that left only the steeple and a few supporting beams. It was the closest thing I can imagine to walking the streets of Nagasaki or Hiroshima after the atomic bombs went off.

That night I met the rest of our team. Our workforce was comprised of a comedian, a nurse, a lady who owned a farm, two teenage boys, a wealthy marketing executive, and two of his employees. The seven castaways on *Gilligan's Island* would probably be better suited for helping the people of Pass Christian. I found it remarkable—we had eight very different individuals with no skills or expertise but who were simply willing to be there.

Before the trip, my father told me, "You're doing a great thing, son. Not everyone can go help." I understood what he meant. However, as I thought about it more and more, I disagreed. I think anyone who really wants to help others can find the time, means, or way to do so. Missionary Neal Maxwell once said, "Don't fear; just live right."

The first morning, we got up around 5:30 and went to the tents where breakfast was served. An old man sat down at the end of our table. His hat bore the words *Veteran of the Korean War.* He told us he was working on his inland home. He stayed with family thirty minutes north, sleeping during the day and working at night. "The heat and humidity here is something like you ain't never had," he said to me in a rusty Cajun voice.

Our first job was to clean the cemetery behind the church. By 10:00 a.m. it felt like it was afternoon. The heat was so intense, it seemed as though I could feel my heart beating inside my head. At some point, we began moving pieces of trees. I pulled one section from the pile and threw it up on my back. Some jagged bark dug into my back. As I pulled it through the rubble, I thought, *I could not imagine being crucified.* Jesus carried much heavier tree pieces up a long, steep hill just so a few guys could nail Him to it. The rough spots of the cross gouged into his back, just after He was gashed forty times with a cat o' nine tails. I thought to myself, *No matter how bad it gets today, it could always be much, much worse.*

We went to a few houses that were still standing to do various chores. The expressions on people's faces were the only things that kept me moving. Everywhere we went we were welcomed warmly and thanked repeatedly. Sometimes the thanks came with hugs and tears. Every person we met had a story.

Upon returning back home, I barely managed to get myself up my stairs to the front porch. I went to the fridge, and before I could open it, I was sitting on the floor of my laundry room, tears running down my face as I remembered those families with coolers in their homes. They had no power and, therefore, no refrigerators, so they went to shelters or inland far enough to get bags of ice and supplies to bring home every day. I love food, but I never thought I would get emotional over a fridge.

Not too long ago, I was in Ethiopia with Compassion. As we visited families in Addis Ababa, we met a lady who lived in the side of a building. She had found a crawl space and placed blankets on the ground for her four kids to sleep on. The space was about six-foot-by-six-foot. It was difficult to imagine two people surviving in this literal hole in the wall. Five people were living in there. As the visit concluded, we asked how we could pray for the family. She responded with a beautiful smile, "Oh, you just thank God for me because I lack nothing."

We are truly fortunate people, and most of us don't even realize it. Yes, we have refrigerators and don't live in crawl spaces, but most of us also have much more to appreciate. We should be thankful for everything from our bodies, to our minds, to our health. We should be thankful for things like rain, music, family, blankets and hobbies. Maureen McCullough said, "My socks may not match, but my feet are always warm." We all have much for which to be thankful.

We aren't blessed because we have houses, cars, and bank accounts. Our resources and material possession don't make us blessed—they make us responsible. We are truly blessed because of Christ and what He has done for us. We are blessed to know and serve one true God and His people.

7

WHAT I LEARNED AT BACHRACH

Keep your face to the sunshine and you cannot see a shadow.
~ Helen Keller

In San Salvador I met a single mom whose daughter had just been sponsored through Compassion. Her daughter was four. They lived together on a rock by a river. Their front door was a box spring, and there were two rooms. There was a small living area with an old cushion-less couch, a chair, and a tiny woodstove. The other room had one bare, twin mattress, where they all slept. The river side of this home was open and had a clothesline that extended through the living room. The roof was an unattached sheet of tin, and the floor was all one slanted, dark gray rock.

The home was in an extremely dangerous area. I noticed shoes hanging from the few power lines that webbed this particular part of town. I asked our driver about them, and he told me that when someone owed another person money and failed to pay, the debtor often disappeared. Then his shoes, the only thing that remained of the now-missing person, were hung up on display to encourage the living to pay their debts.

The air was thick with smells of garbage, rotting meat, and sewage. The heat was visible as it rose off the city streets. Intense arguments taking place in shanties we passed, babies crying everywhere we turned, and the occasional gunshot were the city's soundtrack.

We asked the mother about the dreams she had for her little girl now that she was sponsored by Compassion. She looked confused and told the interpreter she didn't understand. The interpreter said, "She is hopeful that her little girl might eat and be safe." Most of us have dreams for our kids, and those dreams don't usually include the words "eat and be safe." We explained that through Compassion her daughter would eat, be safe, have medical coverage, and even get an education. We asked her what she could envision for her child. Tears running down her face, she said, "I don't know. No one has ever asked me this question."

Think about your life for a few minutes, and your mind should be able to produce countless blessings regardless of your overall life fortunes or mishaps. Recently, I talked to a guy who shared with me all of his lifelong frustrations, expressed his anger about his lack of breaks, and even went to the "where's God?" and "life isn't fair" cards. "Doesn't He know I have needs?" the man said.

I asked, "Needs? How many meals have you missed this week? Will you be able to go home tonight? Will you go there in your own car?"

"Well, yeah, but I want more," he said.

I told him there is a big difference between wants and needs. "Go home tonight to your wife and daughter, then come tell me that God hasn't taken great care of your needs and much, much more."

Jesus speaks to the same type of pessimists in Matthew 6:25–34 (NASB):

For this reason I say to you, do not be worried

> about your life, as to what you will eat or what you will drink; nor for your body, as to what you will put on. Is not life more than food, and the body more than clothing? Look at the birds of the air, that they do not sow, nor reap nor gather into barns, and yet your heavenly Father feeds them. Are you not worth much more than they? And who of you by being worried can add a single hour to his life? And why are you worried about clothing? Observe how the lilies of the field grow; they do not toil nor do they spin, yet I say to you that not even Solomon in all his glory clothed himself like one of these. But if God so clothes the grass of the field, which is alive today and tomorrow is thrown into the furnace, will He not much more clothe you? You of little faith! Do not worry then, saying, "What will we eat?" or "What will we drink?" or "What will we wear for clothing?" For the Gentiles eagerly seek all these things; for your heavenly Father knows that you need all these things. But seek first His kingdom and His righteousness, and all these things will be added to you. So do not worry about tomorrow; for tomorrow will care for itself. Each day has enough trouble of its own.

My first corporate job was with Bachrach menswear, outside Washington, DC. David Nichols, the man who hired me, went on break with me one day. I had had a rough week, selling next to nothing. I have always been transparent, so everyone who saw me that day knew I wasn't happy. David took me into a bookstore in Montgomery Mall and told me to sit down. He walked around the corner and returned shortly thereafter with a book in his hands. "Read this," he said, handing me a children's book. The book was *Did I Ever Tell You How Lucky You Are?* by Dr. Seuss. I sat there reading this book about an old and wise man who tells a wacky story about countless unfortunates whose life circumstances were dreadful. The wise man tells his friend to neither *grumble or stew* because we all have much to be grateful for if we really think about it.

I believe when we are able to appreciate how lucky we really are, service becomes natural. Service impacts lives forever. Katrina helped me understand that in an entirely different light. Sometimes the servant changes more profoundly than the people he serves. From seeing my friend Peter's heroics on a Florida highway to being with Charles in his final hours to experiencing the aftermath of Katrina's devastation, I know that it is our humble availability and willingness to serve that ultimately are most important and fulfilling.

Jesus said in Matthew 20:26–28 (NASB), "It is not this way among you, but whoever wishes to become great among you shall be your servant, and whoever wishes to be first among you shall be your slave; just as the Son of Man did not come to be served, but to serve, and to give His life a ransom for many." Born in a stable, a child of the lower class, and a carpenter by trade, the King of heaven came to touch lepers, wash feet, and lay down his life for us with nails in his hands and feet.

I encourage all to make serving part of daily life. So many people need our help. You may not see the significance of your willingness to be available. Have you ever visited an old folks' home? Have you taken food or communion to a shut-in? Have you mowed lawns, shoveled driveways, or washed cars? Things that seem trivial or small to us are often critical to those in need and usually remembered for life. Charles Shultz, the creator of the *Peanuts* comic strip that features Charlie Brown and Snoopy, was once attached to this philosophy in brilliant fashion…

Charles Schultz Philosophy

Name the five wealthiest people in the world.

Name the last five Heisman trophy winners.

Name the last five winners of the Miss America contest.

Name ten people who have won the Nobel or Pulitzer Prize.

Name the last five Academy Award winners for best actor and actress.

How did you do? The point is, none of us remember the headliners of yesterday. These are no second-rate achievers. They are the best in their fields. Nevertheless, the applause dies, awards tarnish, and trophies are buried with their owners. Here's another quiz. See how you do on this one:

List a few teachers who aided your journey through school.

Name three friends who have helped you through a difficult time.

Name five people who have taught you something worthwhile.

Think of a few people who made you feel appreciated and special.

Think of five people whose company you enjoy.

Easier? The lesson: The people who make a difference in your life are not the ones with the most credentials, the most money, or the most awards. They are the ones that care, the ones who love you.

I know a tale of a Christian camp that inherited an enormous amount of money from an old widow. Her husband, a gifted innovator, died and she was lonely. Her family became complacent and stopped visiting her. They, essentially, were just waiting for her to pass so they could collect. She began walking past the Christian camp every morning for exercise. Every day the kids and people at the camp smile, waved, and talked to this lady. No one knew she was wealthy. When she died, she cited the friendliness of the children in her will and, in essence, wrote out her surviving family and left her fortune to the camp. Words of encouragement, kind deeds, and service are eternally essential for both recipient and servant.

While you live out a life of real love toward those around you, don't neglect your family, job, or leisure time. Don't overload yourself with too many volunteer commitments. God desires us to be servants, but certainly wishes our marriages to prosper and our families to flourish first. Your family should know God is first in your life, but they should never feel they are second to His church or its functions. We all have to say "no" sometimes.

At the same time, don't wait until the end of the year to simply write a check. Katrina would have never impacted my life had I only sent money. When a person sponsors a child through Compassion, the first thing I tell them is to write letters. The financial support changes the child's life prospects, but the emotional investment a person makes in the child's life by writing letters can be immeasurable. When we went to Kenya, my wife and I were able to meet one of our sponsored children, Elizabeth. Despite the schooling, nutrition, and medical benefits she receives through our sponsorship, the first thing she said to us was, "I got your letters." Those letters mean everything to those who have little.

As Dr. Seuss wrote in the book I read while working at Bachrach,"Some critters are much, much, oh, ever so much, much, so muchly, much, much more unlucky than you."

So be grateful. Do something that has meaning and purpose. Taking the time to serve others will provide you with more energy, instead of taking it away. Your life will never be the same once you have experienced the joy of helping others in a healthy manner. You can make a huge difference with the tiniest effort.

8

ME OF LITTLE FAITH

Faith is believing in something when common sense tells you not to.
~ from Miracle on 34th Street

You have weaknesses. The best sports teams and athletes have them. The Death Star had one, Superman had one, and the *Titanic* had one. Sampson, the apostle Paul, and King David had weaknesses. We all do. In 2 Corinthians 12: 9–10 (NIV), Paul writes, "He said to me, 'My grace is sufficient for you, for my power is made perfect in weakness.' Therefore I will boast all the more gladly about my weaknesses, so that Christ's power may rest on me. That is why, for Christ's sake, I delight in weaknesses, in insults, in hardships, in persecutions, in difficulties. For when I am weak, then I am strong." When we acknowledge our weaknesses, His strength becomes perfect in us.

A while back I was serving as an associate minister outside of Tampa, Florida. The job eventually became a worship and youth ministry. I had been there for three years, and the church was growing. I enjoyed being there, but I felt somewhat like I didn't fit in. One day I had a conversation with our most respected elder Ralph. Ralph was in his sixties, retired, and the sacred cow among our leaders. Ralph took me to breakfast every Wednesday morning to talk about his grandchildren, his golf game, and his church. Ralph was a man of integrity, a visionary, and one of the most Christ-like persons I have ever met. Ralph said, "Between you and me, I think you should start looking around for another place to be." I thought I had done something wrong and that he was forewarning me of my eminent firing. Ralph assured me I was doing a great job and told me, "As an elder I'd like to see you stay here for twenty years. As your friend, I see God putting many opportunities in front of you. Just be open."

As the congregation grew larger in number, the church wanted to hire a third staff member. They asked me to choose which role I saw myself in—youth or worship. They also shared concerns that I wasn't completely devoted to the position anymore. They were simply observing weaknesses, as I had grown complacent. I believed in Christ wholeheartedly, but I struggled with doing His will and trusting Him. I knew what God wanted. Each time, however, I thought of every excuse for why I should safely do His will at a more convenient later date. I didn't know what to do.

Growing up, my family went to Ocean City, Maryland, for summer vacation every year. However, when I about eight, my parents decided to go to Myrtle Beach, South Carolina, instead. They showed me the leaflet for the hotel where we would be staying. I immediately noticed the swimming pool, which was a major plus for me. The previous year, while at Ocean City, I had contracted chicken pox. The doctors told my folks I shouldn't be out in the sun. Given that advice, they thought it would be a good idea to go to a movie. We went to see *Jaws*. Good call, Mom and Dad! After watching a twenty-five-foot shark bite people in half for a couple hours, I was *done* with the beach!

The hotel had an Olympic-size pool complete with diving boards and a high dive. I had taken swimming lessons but still felt uneasy swimming in the deep end. My father kept telling me to use the diving board. I explained my hesitance and told him I would try later. This went on all week. Finally, one day my father put his hand on my shoulder and said, "Son, let me help you. I want to tell you something my father told me once." I left all apprehension behind as I anticipated some father-son bonding that would help me overcome my fear. As we walked along the pool deck to the edge of the deep end, my father became very serious. "Son," he said, staring down into the water with his hand still on my shoulder. "Look deep into this pool. Try to focus on the bottom." I concentrated on the shimmering image of the pool floor. "All you need—"

Suddenly the pool water smacked my face. I felt pressure on my lower back where, I realized, my father's other hand had pushed. My father had thrown me in, and I was now going to die. My legs kicked frantically, and my arms flapped like a hyperactive hummingbird. I rose up out of the waters, desperate and furious. As I fought to the edge of the pool, I heard my father laugh, "All you need is a little push!"

I thought, *Yes. And all you need is a lawyer!*

My father taught me how to swim, but that experience taught me something more important. Sometimes, all we need is a push. A nudge. Sometimes it only takes an encouragement, a small success, or one answered prayer to cement our trust in God. It is natural to fear things like deep water, extreme heights, or darkness. The most successful people you know have dealt with fear and doubt in some form or another. It can be difficult, indeed challenging, to achieve a trust in God that leads us to act on faith. It might take place out of desperation. In tense situations that demand fast action, some people demonstrate extreme measures of courage.

In the movie *Indiana Jones and the Last Crusade*, Indiana experienced desperate measures that demanded full-on trust. Indy and his father, Henry, are searching for the Holy Grail. As the plot thickens, Henry suffers a gunshot wound at the hands of the bad guys. Indy realizes his dad has only a few minutes to live. He then faces three tests that will lead him to the Holy Grail if he is successful or certain death if he fails. After successfully completing the first two tests, he walks out onto a ledge overlooking a seemingly bottomless chasm. He reads from his father's notes that the third test requires him to leap from one side of the canyon to the other. As he surveys this jump of what seems to be fifty yards or further, he realizes it is a leap of faith. With his father's life hanging in the balance, Indiana Jones steps out, in faith, into the darkness.

While desperation can produce a stronger faith, I believe acts of trust are just as inspiring when taken out of sheer obedience. Throughout the Gospels, Jesus says these simple words: "Follow me." Jesus says, "Follow me," and turns fishermen, tax collectors, and common men into evangelists, miracle workers, and "fishers of men." Equally as impressive is the faith of these men who dropped everything to follow Him. It is always awesome to witness people who have made drastic lifestyle changes for the cause of Christ. But I find it equally admirable to hear the testimony of people who were raised in the church, learned the ways of Christ, never got into much trouble, loved their parents, were married as a virgin, and preached Christ by the way they live their lives. Both testimonies are beautiful. How awesome is it that two thousand years after he originally said, "Follow me," men still drop everything and do just that?

For people like me, it takes a track record. Mary believed Jesus had risen the moment the angel told her, but Thomas had to see and touch His open wounds to believe. Looking back on my life, the angels in heaven probably refer to me as "Doubting Tony." You know my type: "God, if you just make everything easy and eliminate all manner of risk, I promise I will trust you." At one point or another, most of us have faltered in faith, experienced fear, or shown weakness in one area or another. Just remember, weaknesses are a part of everyone's life but God is in control, and He will help you overcome your perceived shortcomings.

I am sure that some of the disciples, if not all, struggled with faith the same way we do. Sure, they left everything to follow him, but that doesn't mean they didn't have second thoughts or questions at times. We actually see the disciples' phobias all throughout Jesus's ministry. Jesus addresses this in Matthew 8:23–27 (NASB):

> When He got into the boat, His disciples followed Him. And behold, there arose a great storm on the sea, so that the boat was being covered with the waves; but Jesus Himself was asleep. And they came to Him and woke Him,

> saying, "Save us, Lord; we are perishing!" He said to them, "Why are you afraid, you men of little faith?" Then He got up and rebuked the winds and the sea, and it became perfectly calm. The men were amazed, and said, "What kind of a man is this, that even the winds and the sea obey Him?"

Notice the reaction of the disciples. It's as if they were surprised. They magnify their lack of faith with a statement of doubt, even after Christ proved his complete control, even control over Mother Nature. We do the same thing! We wait until the storm is upon us, pray diligently, worry, and then are shocked when we receive answers to our prayers.

Nevertheless, as evident in this story, man's extremity is God's opportunity. When we are at our most desperate hour, God always provides for us. Anyone who sails with Christ in this life experiences storms. Thankfully, storms of doubt and fear can end in a wonderful calm. If Jesus can calm Mother Nature, he can surely manage the worst weather life brings our way.

Still, I had a decision to make. I was about to get married and wasn't sure what I would be doing for a living. I wasn't even sure where I would be living or what I would be doing. Should I just stay on staff and choose a position? Stay safely where I was or step out and trust Him? I was at a major crossroad. And my faith was weak.

9

LEAP, FOCUS, WALK

There are many things that are essential to arriving at true peace of mind, and one of the most important is faith, which cannot be acquired without prayer.

~ John Wooden, Basketball coach

The elders of our church wanted to know my intentions. My decision would be the first step toward the pursuit of new staff. Initially, I had accepted the position to be the worship leader. Youth ministry was a huge need for our church, so I agreed to take that on as well. I loved my youth group. We had nearly quadrupled in size during my tenure, and students were coming for more than the fun stuff, free stuff, or face stuff. I was torn.

One night, I got a call from a guy who wanted me to provide comedy and speak at a camp week that summer in Tennessee. I told him I had used my personal days. "Maybe we can do it next year." I hung up but thought, *How many of these things do you turn down each month?* I had to seriously consider releasing the comfort and security of my weekly paycheck from the church and trust God to provide for me. I didn't want to do that.

I requested a week off to get away and pray about where God wanted me. The elders agreed, and I went home to pack my things for a weeklong getaway. When my suitcase was loaded, I sat down on the steps of my house and prayed. I doubt I have ever prayed longer in one sitting. I prayed for clarity, His will, the youth group, the gift of discernment, and I prayed for the church. I prayed, for the first time, "God, make this obvious to me." That didn't feel like a safe way to pray.

I drove to central Florida that night and prayed the duration of the trip. God was saying, "Just do what I tell you." I thought, *Are you sure?* I kept thinking he would say something different.

I stayed at a youth camp near Lake Wales. I was alone there, because it was off-season. I spent my days praying, shooting basketball, reading, and calling people I most respected for insight. It was a week full of self-evaluation and bearing my soul to God. I'd never prayed with such candor, never been more vulnerable, and never been so frank with God. All week I prayed, "Make it obvious."

All week He said, "Just do what I tell you."

And all week I answered, "Really?" This went on until the following Sunday morning. I prayed, "God, I'm heading back to talk to my elders tonight, are you sure you want me to do this?" Suddenly it was quiet, very quiet. It was so quiet I could barely stand it. I prayed, "If you want to say something else, now is the time!" Nothing.

As God was silent, I started to sweat. Not because of what God told me all week, but because I was facing the reality that I would have to take a leap of faith and trust in God. I was about to get married. I was going to quit my job, start a traveling ministry, and move to Nashville in the course of a few weeks. As I drove out of the camp, I thought, *Am I slap nuts? Is this God? Or is it just me? Is it His will or mine?* Then it happened. I had prayed, "Make it obvious," remember? As I pulled out onto the main road, I noticed an old church with a marquee out front. As I approached it, I read the words that would reinforce my decision and change my life. The sign read as follows…

Leap From the Boat,
Focus,
Walk On Water.

Had I entered *The Twilight Zone*? Remembering the clarity I'd prayed for, I thought, *What's next? Will I find Jesus hitchhiking with a similar message scribbled onto a large piece of cardboard?* How much more plainly could His will be stated? It was impossible to dismiss as coincidence. God had answered my prayers more clearly than I ever expected. The weight of the world fell from my shoulders, as I knew I was following Him. When I break down that old church marquee, several thoughts come to mind…

Leap from the Boat

My father spent two years in the army in late 1960s Vietnam. During high school I tossed around the idea of joining the military. I asked my father what he thought. Dad said, "You better be ready to jump. When they tell you to do something, man, you'd better do it and do it fast!" I thought to myself, *What will I do if they tell me to leap out of an airplane or chopper?* I had visions of being tangled up in my parachute, not being able to open my parachute and, even worse, forgetting my parachute. I envisioned my fall from above with the sound of a whistle in decrescendo as I watched my horrified, plummeting face turn into a little puff of smoke on the ground like Wile E. Coyote in the *The Road Runner* cartoons. It didn't take me long to decide I might not join the army.

We all have or have had someone to answer to in life. At one point or another, each of us has had a boss, teacher, coach, or some type of superior we didn't want to cross or disappoint. I had a college professor who had no tolerance for miscues in his classroom. I traveled on weekends as a college recruiter. Coming home from Minnesota, I got stuck in a blizzard. I had a term paper due the next morning. The college vouched for me, as did elements like the televised newscasts. In fact, I had paid one of the school's secretaries to type my paper the week before (a common practice among men who type like Neanderthals with one finger) so it would be ready for me upon my return. Regardless, he deemed my work late, gave me a zero, and failed me. It wasn't a personal thing either. Mr. Steere had, and has, a great sense of humor and is someone I still call a friend. That said, I never crossed him again.

As a Christian, I am glad God doesn't have a zero tolerance policy for my mistakes. His grace and mercy are two things I might never fully understand. What is even more difficult to understand is why I am sometimes so reluctant to do what he says. When I am honest with myself, it comes down to faith (or lack thereof). When I know God wants me to do something and I don't respond, I can say, "Lord, I trust you," but what I am really saying is, "Lord, I don't trust you" with my actions.

In Matthew 14:25–33, Peter, literally, leaps from the boat (NRSV):

> And early in the morning he came walking toward them on the sea. But when the disciples saw him walking on the sea, they were terrified, saying, "It is a ghost!" And they cried out in fear. But immediately Jesus spoke to them and said, "Take heart, it is I; do not be afraid.'"
>
> Peter answered him, "Lord, if it is you, command me to come to you on the water." He said, "Come." So Peter got out of the boat, started walking on the water, and came toward Jesus. But when he noticed the strong wind, he became frightened, and beginning to sink, he cried out, "Lord, save me!" Jesus immediately reached out his hand and caught him, saying to him, "You of little faith, why did you doubt?" When they got into the boat, the wind ceased. And those in the boat worshiped him, saying, "Truly you are the Son of God."

Peter could've asked safer things of Jesus. He could have said, "Lord, if it is you, may there be a hundred drachma coins in my left tunic pocket." That would've been smart. People view Peter as a failure in this story. At least he did what Jesus told him to do. The only reason he failed was that he took his eyes off Jesus. The moment he stopped trusting, he was in trouble. Even more so than our bosses, coaches, spouses, and superiors, God expects us to do what He says. He will never leave us, steer us in a harmful direction or ask anything of us that we can't handle with His help.

Focus

As a seven year-old rookie in the Federal Little League, I stood at the plate during batting practice with my Kiwanis-sponsored coach, who stood behind me. His arms around my shoulders and hands on my hands, he said, "The key to batting is focus. Wolf, never, never, never take your eye off of the ball." Later, he stood beside me at second base, where I was playing defense. As one of our coaches hit a slow ground ball in our direction, he waited until it bounced off my kneecap into the outfield and said, "Wolf!" I looked at his determined eyes through my own tears, as alert as I could be. "The key to fielding is to never, never, never take your eyes off of the ball." During my eight years in baseball, I became a solid Colt League player, but it was my inability to focus that led to more strikeouts, foul tips, and errors than I care to remember.

One of the most irritating things in the world is when the focus on your camera is off, especially when you have small children. You spend so much time dressing them, getting them into the right position, and convincing them to smile. Then at just the right moment, you push the button and *click!* You go to the computer and download the shot, only to discover the unthinkable. The smiles were vintage, the composition flawless, yet the focus was slightly off. "Uuugghh! For the love of Minolta!" When our focus is even slightly off, our goals and objectives blur. Most cameras and phones have auto-focus now. No matter if it is pitch black, if there is a blinding light, if it's foggy, or if you are underwater—auto-focus kicks in, and the result is usually perfect. I wish I had an auto-focus feature embedded in my psyche. Focus demands a great deal of self-discipline and requires us to set priorities.

In Luke 10:38–42 (MSG), Jesus teaches another lesson in focus:

> As they continued their travel, Jesus entered a village. A woman by the name of Martha welcomed him and made him feel quite at home. She had a sister, Mary, who sat before the Master, hanging on every word he said. But Martha was pulled away by all she had to do in the kitchen. Later, she stepped in, interrupting them. "Master, don't you care that my sister has abandoned the kitchen to me? Tell her to lend me a hand."
>
> The Master said, "Martha, dear Martha, you're fussing far too much and getting yourself worked up over nothing. One thing only is essential, and Mary has chosen it—it's the main course, and won't be taken from her."

Simply put, Jesus tells Martha, "Mary is doing that which is most important." If you ask yourself that question throughout the day, you're likely to answer "No" without focus.

Focus is about prioritizing. Prioritizing enables

us to develop positive changes in behavior and mindset so that we maintain that which is, in fact, most important. Ask God for wisdom and to make the most vital things obvious. Ask Him to help you focus on the things that are most important as you begin each day.

Walk on Water

When I hear the phrase "walk on water," I immediately think of Jesus. Then I think about extraordinary people with incredible stories. Names like Helen Keller, Ludwig van Beethoven, and Joni Eareckson Tada come to mind. Suffice to say, tales of hearing impaired composers and paraplegic artists inspire us all. Then I think of Peter. Peter is the only other person we know of in history who literally did walk on water. Peter wasn't an Olympian or magician. Aside from the fact that he spent three years with Jesus, Peter was as ordinary as you and I. You might think, *Jesus made that happen.* You would be half correct. Without faith in Christ, Peter would've never stepped out.

God's word tells us we have the same power. Philippians 4:13 (NKJV) promises, "I can do all things through Christ who strengthens me." God hears our prayers and knows we desire to be the best we can be for Him. I believe discernment comes from the Spirit in regard to what we are supposed to do for God. When we believe and trust in Him enough to let Him work on and in us, our ability to see is immediately unclouded.

I had some reasonable excuses to explain to God why I wasn't doing His will. "We're about to get married. We're making decent money. We like Florida. We don't know anyone in Nashville. Maybe this is my will, not His." What I was really saying was, "God, I don't think you can meet my needs. I doubt you will bless me and my new wife. I'm not convinced you will pour out your blessings, even though you said you would." I was thirty-three years old, a practicing minister, yet, lack of faith was my biggest weakness. God's word, however, encourages us in the midst of our shortcomings.

God constantly speaks to us through His word, His people and, occasionally, old church marquees. Hearing him and discerning His will is a lifelong process. It doesn't come without heartbreak, mistakes, and failures. Believe me, I have tripped up in every area of my life at one point or another. Babe Ruth, as great as he was, struck out more times than any other player in baseball history. You will struggle at times, you'll fall, and you'll wonder if you're going to drown now and again. You will also have many joys along the way. Accept and embrace your weaknesses and strengths. Leap. Focus. Walk. Be open to His plan, and develop the ability and willingness required to act on your faith. Be completely honest with yourself and with God as your quest for authenticity takes place.

10

THE INFAMOUS "BOOG-A- LOO"

You were born an original; don't die a copy.
~ John Mason, English Army Major

In June 1987, I met an extraordinary man. I was touring with Son's Up that summer. We traveled the East Coast with a full forty-man roster of teenage singers, actors, and tech guys. We performed at churches most nights, but occasionally, we played camps or conventions. One night we played at a small camp outside of Richmond, Virginia. Oak Hill Christian Service Camp was one of the most pitiful, unsanitary facilities to ever host camp weeks for humans. There are missionaries who wouldn't stay at this camp. It wouldn't pass inspection if the government were ever aware of its existence. Dilapidated structures, poisonous snakes, and a guy who wandered the woods in a hockey mask were never part of the camp brochure. The camp mascot was a three-legged dog, named Tripod. And I'm pretty sure the camp was built on an Indian burial ground. Despite all of this, incredible ministry always seemed to take place there. So many people have poured so much love and many resources into it over the years. Oak Hill *still* holds a dear place in my heart.

However, the most bizarre thing about this camp was a guy named Mark "Boog-a-loo" Lukhard. He sat in the front row during our performance. He and his friend Jeff were about as hard to notice as a five-hundred-pound senior citizen dancing around a water sprinkler in nothing but an undersized diaper. Mark and Jeff looked as if they'd just came off the set of Michael Jackson's "Beat It" video. Jeff wore an outfit that might have been designed by the Glad trash bag people and jewelry rivaled only by Mr. T. Mark was even more striking. Prince could have switched clothes with Mark and neither would have looked any different. Amid a plethora of chains, studs, and earrings, Mark's hair stood erect in every direction imaginable. You almost expected him to say, "Cock-a-doodle-do," whenever he spoke. I thought to myself, *This guy must be a huge Foghorn Leghorn fan.* Mark and Jeff were unique to say the very least.

Mark and Jeff laughed, clapped, and danced throughout our show that night. I wasn't sure what they would think, but they really enjoyed it. As we were tearing down our equipment and loading our bus, a camp staffer said, "You guys are welcome to attend our bonfire service. There's a guy speaking tonight that you really need to hear." When we got to the bonfire, the scene was typical. A couple college students with a guitar and tambourine led the hundred or so campers, mostly high-school students, singing songs of the "Kumbaya" variety. What happened next was *not* typical.

Emerging from the surrounding woods came an ear-piercing chant. "Give me a J!" A voice shrieked to the eager teens.

They all responded with a roar that echoed off the trees, "J, you got your J, you got your J!" As expectations built to a frenzy, the chanting continued to "E," "S," "U," and another "S." Seconds later the name of Jesus was being bellowed out against the woods in perfect time like the chorus of "We Will Rock You" by Queen. Mark's silhouette came into view from the woods, with energy unlike anything I had ever experienced. He circled the campfire as he preached, and the light struck his face as he turned. When he faced me, I saw an intensity that was both commanding and intimidating. As he continued to walk around the fire, I saw his back, which made him appear to be a stalking shadow. This was the perfect contrasting stage for the young evangelist, who so passionately preached about light and darkness.

As he continued to recite passage after passage without a Bible, words like "revolution," "uprising," and "eternity" amplified with the same type of power and energy that booms from an electric guitar at a rock concert. I watched in stunned silence as people came forward, bowing, praying, and even weeping. Demons scattered from the fire into the blackness of the forest that night. Mark was the most authoritative speaker I had ever heard. The amazing thing, however, was while he preached a message filled with hellfire and brimstone, there was no hate in it. I felt as though he genuinely loved every person there, including me. That night, twenty or so young people gave their lives to Christ, which was becoming routine following Mark's sermons.

That summer, Mark and I became friends. I was amazed at what God was doing through his testimony. Mark had led a rough life, leaving home at a young age in complete rebellion. He developed a talent for break dancing and rapping, as the hip-hop culture grew in the early '80s. This would serve as a virtual passport into places preteens ordinarily and legally could not go. Mark began "working" to liven the atmosphere and enhance the profits of many clubs in the Richmond, Virginia, area. This is where Mark met Jeff, whose story was very similar. They attempted to fill themselves via their God-given talents instead of relying on God himself. Mark and Jeff found themselves in the middle of more fights, alcohol, girls, and drugs than you can fathom. They were popular, independent, making money, and living "the life," but something wasn't complete.

In the summer of 1987, something happened. "We came to the Lord and to our senses, as a result of Jeff's praying mom," Mark recalled.

Jeff's mom was a prayer warrior. One day she got an idea: "I dare you two to go to Christian camp this summer." They laughed. They thought, *Oh, sure, we'll fit right in. Christians love guys with Mohawks, tattoos, and piercings. This will be great!* However, it was a bet, and after all, who wants to lose a dare to their mother?

Mark remembers, "By the grace of God, we thought, OK. *Let's go to camp. Let's go mess with the Christians!*" They planned to go, win the bet, be a complete disruption and irritate as many Christians as they could. God had other plans.

Upon arriving on Sunday night, they really believed they would be kicked out in a few days or hours. "We had a mind-set," Mark recalls. "We always did everything to the extreme. Whatever we did, we did all-out. Everything from our dress to our hair to our speech was screaming out, 'Look at us!' We fully expected to be ostracized within the first hour."

In the registration area, the camp manager

Glenn Foster greeted them. Glenn looked like an honest-to-goodness, *The Dukes of Hazzard*–watchin', American flag–wavin', pickup truck–drivin', country music–listenin', cornstalk-growin' good ol' boy. Mark knew a ticket home was inevitable, but God was already at work. Glenn was not what he seemed. Glenn was a sold-out, compassionate, loving, and devoted follower of Jesus. Love oozed from Glenn's pores. To their complete shock, Glenn made them feel right at home. Mark and Jeff were welcomed without so much as a sideways look.

A young man named Scott Browning introduced himself. Scott sincerely tried to talk to them. He didn't judge, and it was completely transparent to Mark and Jeff. This wasn't surface chitchat. This was genuine "I care about you" stuff. That night, based on Scott's approach and Glenn's acceptance, Mark and Jeff decided to really give the camp an honest chance. As the rest of the week went by, more and more students approached them. As they interacted, they felt loved like never before. As performers Mark and Jeff often gained admiration for their talents, but this was different. This was an unconditional love for no apparent reason. It humbled Mark. "Despite all the crazy things we had been into, we felt that, at the very least, we were on equal terms with everyone else," he admits.

That week, Mark and Jeff had given their lives to Christ. In one week, they had gone from, "Let's go mess with the Christians," to, "Let's become Christians." That quickly turned into, "Let's go make Christians!" Upon their conversion, Mark and Jeff went just as radical with their newfound faith as they had with their haircuts and baggy pants. Locking and popping (see the '80s guide-to-break-dancing dictionary) shifted into studying and preaching. Mark and Jeff promptly returned to their old stomping grounds to share the good news. However, clubs full of hip-thrusting youngsters aren't always receptive to the idea that they need Jesus.

Mark recalls, "One time we actually beat a guy down for making fun of our testimony." Fistfighting for Jesus usually falls somewhat ineffective in evangelism. Nothing says "love" like a knuckle sandwich and a kick in the crotch. While some crowds were unreceptive, others were inspired and energized by these revolutionaries and their challenges.

Mark and Jeff were just being who God made them to be. They preached hard, studied fanatically, wrote, and recorded hip-hop music to express their zeal. Mark says, "If that's your heart and you sincerely say to God, 'Here I am, use me,' you'd better fasten your seat belt." Being different usually draws criticism. It was as true in Jesus's time as it is today. Jesus was different. So different, in fact, that a nation wanted His blood. His disciples were different. Peter was just a redneck fisherman who would've been excited about Mark and Jeff's Fistfights-for-Jesus program. Then there was Paul, a man of high culture who, after his conversion, turned countercultural. When you swim upstream in the church, people talk about you. They might offend and even dislike or express hatred toward you. Mark recently reflected on his first days as an excited young evangelist, "We may have done things differently, but one thing is certain: We were going do *something* because we were chasing after

God."

To this day, Mark is one of my closest friends. He and Jeff had a profound impact on my life. Mark and Jeff's legacy will stand with the thousands of young people who first met Jesus through his sermons. "Serve One" can sometimes mean serving someone very close to you. Mark and Jeff were lucky to have mothers who never gave up on them. Their moms were prayer warriors who loved their boys unconditionally. They both had mothers who believed their sons' lives had purpose. Even when their boys were living as a couple of promiscuous hell-raisers, these ladies loved and prayed for their sons.

11

ESPECIALLY YOU

The privilege of a lifetime is being who you are.
~ Mythologist Joseph Campbell

Please keep being who *you* are. God made you uniquely for a reason. He wants to speak through you to specific people for specific reasons. We should be more concerned about being real than saying and doing "all the right things." People might not always agree with you, but if you are being real, they will respect you. Dr. Seuss, a man who embraced his distinctiveness, said, "Be who you are, and say what you feel, because those who mind don't matter, and those who matter don't mind." God created you, exclusively, to be who you are and to share your story. He can use you in a mighty way. You are special. I implore you, please, stay that way.

Authenticity is an incredible and beautiful thing. If your eyes were green instead of blue, you wouldn't be you. If you didn't have your great sense of humor, you wouldn't be you. If you hadn't failed the first time you tried something challenging (and the second time), you wouldn't be you. If you hadn't experienced that heartache a while back, you wouldn't be you. If you hadn't had children, you wouldn't be you. If you hadn't heard those words of encouragement years ago, you wouldn't be you. If God made you anyone else, you wouldn't be you. Why we try to do what everyone else does, I don't know. Why we are scared to be ourselves, I don't know. At the core of this enigma is the old saying, "The biggest obstacle anyone has to overcome is their own attitude about themselves."

I've often heard preachers say, "God doesn't *need* you." I understand why they are saying that, and I recognize that God can do whatever he has to do in order to accomplish His tasks with or without us. However, I think our willingness to serve and allow Him to work through us is something He loves. In Luke 15:4–7 (NIV), Jesus tells the Pharisees just how important we, even "sinners," are to God:

> Suppose one of you has a hundred sheep and loses one of them. Doesn't he leave the ninety-nine in the open country and go after the lost sheep until he finds it? And when he finds it, he joyfully puts it on his shoulders and goes home. Then he calls his friends and neighbors together and says, "Rejoice with me; I have found my lost sheep." I tell you that in the same way there will be more rejoicing in heaven over one sinner who repents than over ninety-nine righteous persons who do not need to repent.

Maybe God doesn't need us but, make no mistake, He loves you more than you can imagine. Think about the story of creation in Genesis. God created all things, named them, and gave them different qualities, sounds, colors, and abilities. In the beginning, God came up with, and made, the heavens and the earth. He thought up and made light, dark, the waters, the heavens, the sun, the moon, sea creatures, birds, creeping things, and beasts of the field. God made every diverse sound—growls, screeches, grunts, roars, and yaps—and he liked what he heard. He created colors, and painted the earth with a palette of hues and tints, too many to consider. He mixed and splattered, stroked and brushed with an artistic mastery beyond compare, and he liked what he saw.

Then, on the sixth day, God went one step further. Genesis 1:26–31 says this:

> Then God said, "Let us make mankind in our image, in our likeness, so that they may rule over the fish in the sea and the birds in the sky, over the livestock and all the wild animals, and over all the creatures that move along the ground."
>
> So God created mankind in his own image, in the image of God he created them; male and female he created them.
>
> God blessed them and said to them, "Be fruitful and increase in number; fill the earth and subdue it. Rule over the fish in the sea and the birds in the sky and over every living creature that moves on the ground.'"
>
> Then God said, "I give you every seed-bearing plant on the face of the whole earth and every tree that has fruit with seed in it. They will be yours for food. And to all the beasts of the earth and all the birds in the sky and all the

> creatures that move along the ground—everything that has the breath of life in it—I give every green plant for food." And it was so.
>
> God saw all that he had made, and it was very good.

Notice the last sentence. God creates all week long and says, "It is good," at the end of each day. However, at the end of day six, God had given life to creation in His own likeness (you and me) and He says, "It is *very* good." Above the beauty of the canyons, the brilliance of the sun, and the depths of all the galaxies of the universe, you are the pride of His creation. Truly, He saved His best for last. You!

You are like a dishwasher. It's true. When I was twenty-eight years old, I was working as a youth minister in North Carolina. A month before moving, I looked at apartments. The lady showing me the various layouts and options took me inside a two-bedroom, third-floor apartment with a great view. The best part was when she showed me the kitchen. "This is your dishwasher," she said.

"Dishwasher?" I asked, having never had one in my previous rentals or at home while growing up. Actually, growing up, I *was* the dishwasher.

"You're going to love this!" she said, while demonstrating. She opened the door and pointed to a little box. "You just squirt your soap in here, shut the door, and that's it! When you pull those dishes out, you'll be able to see your own reflection on your plates."

"I'll take the apartment," I said, before we

even talked about price.

"Twenty-eight-year old bachelor" often translates into "idiot" around the kitchen. I bought soap, just like the lady said, to put into my dishwasher. In hindsight, I probably should have bought dishwasher detergent. What I bought was more like liquid hand soap. I put my dishes in, squirted some soap into the box, shut the door, and went into my living room to watch television. After a few minutes, out of the corner of my eye, I saw a large white object seeping out of my kitchen. I ran in to find a giant "suds monster" rapidly approaching and gaining strength. I was quickly reminded of a movie from my childhood—*The Blob*. Armed only with a dishrag and a Slim Jim, I attacked The Blob head on. I somehow managed to find the "cancel" button on the dishwasher, and the creature was defeated.

Most people would have just gone back to the store and bought the right stuff. Not me. My kitchen was already a mess, so I thought, "I wonder what would happen if I put mustard in there?" I sprung into action, nearly giddy over the vision of a yellow giant beast crawling from the bowels of my dishwasher. However, much to my dismay, fifteen minutes after the operation, there were no signs of life. I crept, petrified, toward the dishwasher with one arm extended in the direction of the growling machine. Against my better judgment, I opened the door in midcycle. The rumbling ceased and steam emerged. Then it hit me, the nastiest stench imaginable. Dr. Frankenstein's fiendish creation sewn of dead humans couldn't have smelled this bad. I pulled one plate from the depths of ground zero. Covered in a slimy, golden, mustardy film, the plate completely reeked. It was disgusting.

After I tried the same experiment with mayonnaise and grape jelly, I returned to Walmart to purchase some Palmolive dishwasher detergent. It worked wonderfully! I pulled out a plate, held it up to the light, and actually could see myself! God has made you the same way. He created in you a place in your heart designed as his abode. This space is for God alone. Unfortunately, we often fill it with all the wrong things. We use everything from money to earthly relationships to hobbies to, in some cases, things that are incredibly detrimental. When we place anything else but God in the center of our being, it's a lot like putting mustard in a dishwasher. The mess can be unbelievable—but avoidable.

God is crazy about you! In Colossians, Paul calls us "God's chosen people." The book of Romans tells us that as God's children we are "heirs of God and co-heirs with Christ." I Peter says, that you are a part of a "called generation." Ephesians says we are his "dearly loved children." Beyond words, God esteems us with such great love and compassion. He sent to Earth His only child, who resurrected for us. God desires to fill the void in your life and be the center. He loves you no matter what you did yesterday, last week, or last year. No matter what you did twenty years ago, no matter what you did earlier today, He loves you for the rest of your days.

One of the happiest moments of my life was the day I became a father. The moment our doctor delivered Brooklyn and held her up, Laura said, "Look, your chin!" Brooke had a small dimple on her chin, just like mine. She had my chin. I was in love the moment I saw her. Now that I have three lovely little girls and a son, nothing makes my day happier than when a stranger sees us together and says, "Your kids are beautiful. They look just like you." You know, "beautiful" is not typically the first word people use to describe me! Nonetheless, I love it when people tell me that. I'm a proud dad.

So is God. Your heavenly Father feels that same way about you. The moment He created you, He was in love. He proved that love for you two thousand years ago when He placed His only child on this earth with an objective that would lead to resurrection and ascension. When God created you, He decided you were so special that He sent Jesus to demonstrate life everlasting. You are designed like a dishwasher, sort of. God wants to be in the soap dish, and He wants to permeate every corner and crevasse of your life. As cheesy as this may sound, His desire is to hold you up to the light and see His reflection. He desires to see Himself in you.

God wants others to see Him through you too. He has positioned many people in your life who need someone just like you to talk to, share with, and truly understand and empathize. Every time someone calls you and asks for help, you have a chance to impact that person. You can affect them in a positive way and allow God to minister to them through you, or refuse and adversely affect them eternally. You have an awesome responsibility. You can reach people I will never meet, people your minister will never know. Your circle of people, places, and things is unique. Your gifts, talents, and personality are too. That said, the exceptional ability and persona you possess are meant to be share with those around you. Psychiatrist and author David Viscott perfectly broadcast this truth when he said, "The purpose of life is to discover your gift; the meaning of life is to give it away."

In your authenticity and uniqueness, God has a plan for your life. He always has. He desires to use you, your special stories, and your experiences to serve the world.

Before the foundations of this world were laid
Before the omnipotence of God was displayed
Before all creation, before the start of time
Our Father had you in mind.

And He made the springtime so earth could renew
Then painted the fall seasons beautiful view
When you were created, creation was through
And He made you special, especially you.

~ Son's Up

12

DECIDING TO SERVE

The best way to find yourself is to lose yourself in the service of others.
~ Mahatma Gandhi

A few years ago, I was on a road trip when I watched the movie *Pay It Forward* in my hotel room. The movie is about a boy who works on a school assignment that leads to social changes that spread from city to city. Assigned to come up with some idea that will improve mankind, the boy decides if he can do three good deeds for someone and they, in turn, can "pay it forward" and so forth, unprecedented positive changes can occur. The boy does his three deeds, time passes, and the boy believes his experiment is a failure. Little does he know a geometric avalanche of love and kindness cascades through the city and even beyond. If you or I were successful in pulling off the "Pay it Forward" idea ourselves, the first time we would reach three people. That is not a staggering number. The second time, we would impact nine. That's good. By the third time, twenty-seven people would be touched in a special way. The fifth time 243 people would be changed, the ninth time nearly 20,000, and by the sixteenth time, 43 million people would be reached in a positive way.

In contrast to such ethical rudders as "give them what they deserve," or even "an eye for an eye," this movie's message was the opposite of what most moviegoers usually applaud. However, think about it—the notion of treating people with love, regardless of whether they deserve it, isn't all that novel. Jesus instructed His twelve disciples in Matthew 10:8 (NIV), "Freely you have received; freely give." Jesus wanted the twelve to pay forward the fruit of the blessings they had received. He expects the same from us.

In Romans 5:6–8 (NIV), Paul writes, "At just the right time, when we were still powerless, Christ died for the ungodly. Very rarely will anyone die for a righteous person, though for a good person someone might possibly dare to die. But God demonstrates his love for us in this: While we were still sinners, Christ died for us." God actively sought after our best interests, even though we didn't deserve it. Now that Christ has transformed us, what are we supposed to do?

And we are not limited to three random acts of kindness. There is no limit to what you can do for the cause of Christ. There are no scriptures or commands that regulate the amount of times we are able to serve. God doesn't wish to curb your good deeds. He wants you to be you, to serve and bless many. You don't have to be on staff at the local church to evangelize your community for the cause of Christ. You just have to be available, willing, and ready. God doesn't always call the qualified, but God always qualifies those who are called.

What qualifications did Gideon have? In chapter six of Judges we find out that before delivering the Midianites, he was hiding under a winepress assuming God had abandoned him and his people. What qualifications did Jephthah have? In Judges, chapter 11, we learn he was the son of a whore, his brothers rejected him, and he associated with the wrong kinds of people and made foolish vows. What qualifications did David have? He was physically tiny, and a musician who was "prudent in speech." That sounds more like the resume of a pixie than that of a giant-slayer. What qualifications did Peter have? Peter was a hotheaded fisherman who denied Jesus to his face in his most crucial hour. What qualifications did Paul have? Paul was a killer of Christians and persecutor of the church. God has called you to do work for Him, to use your talents for him. God wants you to serve him. You are qualified.

I want to challenge you to take advantage of every opportunity you can, every day, to simply serve. Ask yourself these questions:

Is there someone I can help?
Is there a gift I'm not using?
Has God blessed me with some talent I have buried?
Have numerous people commented on one of my strengths?
Might that be a message from God about His will for my life?
Do my neighbors know me as someone they can turn to for help?
Do people at work come to me for advice or guidance?
Do they know I am a Christian?
Does anyone know about my Christianity?

How will your story read when your life is over? What will your legacy be? More important, what will Jesus see in you? What will God think of your life, and what you have done with it?"

Initially I thought this would be a great spot in my book for a story about some legendary servant for the cause of Christ. Maybe a story about a selfless crusader known throughout the world for his or her faithful service would be moving. Perhaps a reminder from scripture about how one of God's many biblical heroes would serve as a motivator. Instead, I decided to tell you three stories you have never heard before about several people you have never heard of, people who are doing things the world might view as insignificant. The following stories involve servants who have no theological degrees or phenomenal talents yet are making a huge difference in this world by serving God.

John Norman

One of my classmates in college was an anomalous person. John Norman was the very definition of mild-mannered. To this day, I doubt I have ever met a more unassuming person. I first discovered John wasn't your typical person my sophomore year, one night when Mike Tyson was fighting on Pay-per-view. For a Bible college, there were an unnatural number of boxing fans in our dorm and on campus. School librarian Cheryl Lindsley and her husband, Rich, were even into it. All the guys from the dorm gathered at the Lindsley house on fight nights. We each chipped in a couple bucks to pay for the fight and order some pizza. On this particular night, however, the Lindsleys were going away for the weekend.

John said, "My mom will let us come watch it

at our house." John's family lived about an hour north of campus, so we all loaded up in nine or ten vehicles and followed John toward Virginia Beach. John was the first guy on campus to buy a Yugo. He bought it used and wrecked from a salvage yard. We trailed John's little white toaster-on-wheels off the highway into a less-than-wealthy area. We silently began to respect John more, as we realized where he'd come from to attend Bible college. We knew John was financially poor, but this was shocking. At a red light, we watched the police cuff a young man on the other side of the street in front of a liquor store. Right about then, that theme song from television's *S.W.A.T.* series started bouncing around in my head.

Just as we had locked all our car doors and asked God to "deliver us," the streets cleared and we saw signs of comfort and hope on the horizon. At first, there were some convenience stores, fast-food joints, and car dealerships. Then we passed some very nice subdivisions. We breathed easier as we watched John's miniscule imitation automobile turn left into an unbelievable neighborhood. These houses looked more like castles than homes. One guy in our car said, "He must be lost. Maybe he's asking for directions." John's little car sputtered into the circular driveway of a palatial three-story mansion. He stepped out of his car and motioned us all to follow him. "No way," we whispered simultaneously.

John called, "Come on in, guys. It's all right."

Now hold your stinkin' horses, I thought to myself. *I have bought meals for this guy at Taco Bell a couple times!* I watched as the front door opened, and his sister and mom emerged. They hugged him and walked him in through the front door (into the grand foyer in this case). We followed in stunned silence. The front room had all-white furniture, tall bookshelves, marble floors, and a white baby grand piano that was stunning. "Who plays piano, John?" I asked.

"No one," John said. The piano was part of the decor. Just past the piano room was something I had never seen in a house before: an elevator. While a few of our guys walked out on the pier to see the Normans' boat—they lived on a small lake)—the rest of us followed John into his parents' entertainment room. George Lucas would have been blown away by this technological wonder. It was astonishing.

The only thing more amazing to me was John. I had known John for several years and never dreamed he was from a family with money. John refused to take any of his father's money when he left for college—he wanted to make his own way. John took out student loans and waived on the prestigious educational institutions his family had access to, to pursue God's calling to ministry. What I do remember are his solemn and meek demeanor and consistent joy I saw from John over the years. Every time someone needed something, John popped up. Anytime there were opportunities to serve, to assist even one person, John was there. I saw in John the reflection of Christ.

Tiffany and Crystal

During my youth ministry years, I tried to plan numerous service projects and occasional missions trip. My kids did a lot of work over the years. Painting buildings, cleaning parking lots, raking leaves, or shoveling snow for the elderly or shut-in were the norm. However, the service projects were never the point. It wasn't really even as much for the recipients of the efforts. These acts of kindness, both planned and random, were more about life lessons and teachable moments that occurred during the deeds. If you want to have a positive influence on youth, laugh with them, hang out with them, and play with them. If you truly want to teach them and establish unbreakable links among yourselves, model service and serve with them. When they see you serve, they see Jesus.

One Thanksgiving, I was visiting elderly folks in the hospital. Our senior minister was visiting family in Kentucky and asked me to go by the hospital on Thanksgiving Day. As it became late afternoon and all my visits had wrapped up, I walked down the hall toward the exits. Tiffany Noesges and Crystal Orta approached me. Tiffany and Crystal were two of my senior-high students. They were carrying fully cooked turkeys on a cart. "What are you guys doing here?" I asked.

"We do this for the elderly every year," they said.

"Visit the hospital?" I asked.

"No, we do that every week. But every year on Thanksgiving, we try to take turkeys to the ones we know are alone."

Suddenly, I was in a beautiful field, green and yellow with daisies, under a powder-blue sky. John Denver waved at me and played his guitar. A choir of angels appeared on the hillside, and I found myself skipping barefoot in a white gown. Surrounding me, dancing arm in arm in merriment, were Tiffany,

Crystal, the thawed headless turkeys, an old fat guy in a leotard, the Dallas Cowboys Cheerleaders, my friend Kevin Barton, and the Indian from the Village People. Bluebirds circled, and smiles were on the faces of all as we sang the chorus of The Beatles' "All You Need Is Love."

I opened my eyes, and I was back in the hospital, facing Tiffany and Crystal again. "Hey! Are you all right?" Tiffany asked.

As I returned from Neverland, I smiled. "I'm fine. I'm good. I'm OK."

They looked at me as if to say, "Our youth minister is a dork." I looked at them thinking, *They get it. I am looking at two angels. I am truly in God's presence here.* They could have been anywhere on that Thanksgiving Day, but Tiffany and Crystal were putting strangers ahead of themselves. I felt such admiration for them—you know, the kind of admiration a kid usually has for his dad or coach or youth leader. Until the day I die, I will look up to Tiffany Noesges and Crystal Orta.

The Gettigs

A few years ago, I led worship at Sylvan Hills Christian Camp, just north of the metropolis of Howard, Pennsylvania. My good friend Wes McElravy was the dean of a small camp week at Sylvan Hills for about fifty junior-high students. I arrived on Sunday night, got all of my sound equipment and instruments set up, and went to a staff meeting. Camp weeks like this one enlist volunteers and youth ministers from various churches in the area to supervise and work with the students. On this particular staff, there were three remarkable people who would, over the course of the next few years, impact my life as well as many youth at the camp, as well as others at their churches and communities.

The first guy I met was Scott Gettig. Scott had a soft spot in his heart for kids. Aside from the fact that he has a van full of his own kids, his interaction with them was more natural than some youth pastors I know. It came as no surprise to learn Scott was a schoolteacher. All week his love for youth and for Christ was palpable. His sense of humor and teachings were equally superb. In addition, despite his joking spirit, the students smiled at him with admiration. Students can spot an authentic adult a mile away. But they can spot a fake from even farther. Scott obviously understood two things. First, as a teacher giving his free weeks away to a group of adolescent pranksters in cabins without air-conditioning in the middle of nowhere, he understood service. Moreover, he understood goodness is caught more than it is taught. Scott had a sister on staff too.

Anita Tressler (formerly Anita Gettig) was the camp nurse. Anita wasn't just a nurse at camp; nursing was her occupation. Anita was behind the scenes, organizing kids' meds as they checked in and filling out forms but, by day's end, I was taken aback by her. Wes asked me to lead singing at the campfire at night that week, including a traditional closing song. They told me, "Anita will sing it if you just play. She's used to singing it unaccompanied."

As the campfire ended, I found Anita and said, "I'll just listen tonight so I can get a feel for it." The first note caught my ear, and the second caught my heart. What in the world was a voice like that doing out in this murkiness? Obscurity is a place for mediocre singers like my dad, not Anita. *She belongs performing on a stage or in a studio*, I thought. Why wasn't she pursuing singing professionally? By week's end, I realized she was in her concert hall, right where she was. God desires the heartfelt utilization of our gifts for the good of others. Anita is a great singer and an accomplished nurse. She is also the mother of three, including a son Eric. Eric has special needs, and I am convinced Anita is on this earth to love and serve him. She loves her kids equally, but her face lights up in a special way when she talks about Eric. Anita was a servant, using her gifts and knowledge where they belonged.

Finally, just before campfire, another Gettig showed up. Andy Gettig stands six-foot-three or so. He looks like he could line up with five offensive linemen and catch a short pass over the middle while avoiding a few linebackers. Instead of an NFL tight end, Andy is a full-time firefighter. Andy is the youngest brother. Andy is kind of like a "baby big brother." Andy spoke at campfire each night. Andy wasn't a dynamic Mark Lukhard by any stretch. Yet, to my surprise, Andy had his own charisma. His messages were personal and very insightful. Watching him play volleyball, direct games, and sit with the youth all week enabled everyone who encountered him to see him in a very different light than his physical traits would suggest.

Most guys with Andy's brawn are more easily imagined delivering a knockout punch than a touching message. Throwing lumber or steel around would seem more picturesque for Andy than throwing his arm around a troubled child. Most guys with Andy's skills would be anywhere else than an old Christian service camp in the middle of summer. Andy was also a servant. Imagine that. A schoolteacher, a nurse, and a firefighter—service isn't just a Sunday morning thing with the Gettigs. Serving is what they do with their lives, their vocations, and their faith.

What makes a servant serve? What makes some people put others first, while others never do? What makes one man consider others, while another man puts his own desires first? A decision. It all comes down to an everyday, every-opportunity choice. That decision comes for those who seem to have an absolute resolve for service as much as it does for those of us who struggle with selflessness. We all determine whether we will be givers or takers. By our own choices, each of us either says, "More of you and less of me," or "More for me and less for you, Jesus." Servants understand that they can be the "hands and feet" of Christ when they see an unfulfilled need around them. Servants know "a man can't just sit around." If you want to do something special, you have to *do* something.

To quote hospitality mogul J.W. Marriott Jr., you have to "decide to decide." Serve one, or serve none.

13

GO BE JESUS

Setting an example is not the main means of influencing others; it is the only means.
~ Physicist Albert Einstein

On July 2, 1982, Larry Walters decided to do something. Larry was from San Pedro, California. Larry always dreamed of flying but was unable to become a pilot due to his bad eyesight. Regardless, Larry was determined to fly. He came up with an unorthodox plan when he was young. The flight idea included weather balloons, a lawn chair, a few sandwiches, and a pellet gun. No matter how you add all of these items up, it equals a bad idea. Walters and his girlfriend bought forty-five four-foot weather balloons and helium tanks at California Toy Time Balloons. To avoid suspicion, they forged requisition from his employer, Film Fair Studios, saying the balloons were for a television commercial shoot. That is when the fun began.

Walters attached the balloons to his lawn chair, filled them with helium, donned a parachute, and prepared for his flight. He took one "carry-on bag," including a pellet gun, a CB radio, a few sandwiches, soft drinks, and a camera. Unfortunately, when his friends cut the rope that tied his lawn chair to his jeep, Walters's took off much quicker than anyone had anticipated. Larry figured that, given his weight and other estimates, he would rise a hundred feet above the ground. He miscalculated. In a matter of minutes, Larry and his lawn chair were two thousand feet off the ground and drifting over Long Beach. Larry eventually passed through the primary approach corridor of the Long Beach Airport. Planes flew past him, over him, and under him. How funny would that be? Imagine being on a plane and looking out the window: "There's the Pacific Ocean. There's the Staples Center. Oh, and, there's a guy in a lawn chair!"

After a few hours in flight, Larry got the nerve to shoot a few balloons. He actually descended somewhat slowly. His landing might have been perfect if not for the power lines. Larry's dangling cables tangled in some power cables, which caused a neighborhood blackout in Long Beach for about twenty minutes. Larry, however, managed to climb down to the ground safely from his tied-up "Air Chair." When reporters finally made it to Larry, they frantically asked questions. After hearing Larry's story and dream to fly, one reporter asked, "Larry, why did you do it?" Larry replied, "A man can't just sit around."

We can't just sit around. Our legacy, as imitators of Christ, would be hollow without serving. Our example to those who know we are Christians is hypocrisy without selfless action. James 1:27 (NIV) says, "Religion that God our Father accepts as pure and faultless is this: to look after orphans and widows in their distress and to keep oneself from being polluted by the world." Without doing what Christ asks us to do or following his teaching, we are merely that, good people. With remorse, I know I don't do enough. I know there are needs all around me. My trips with Compassion International have shown me that needs exist all over this world. Mother Teresa brought some perspective to what we can do when she said, "If you can't feed one hundred people, feed one."

We can't just sit around. In John 21:15–17 (NIV), Jesus makes this point clear with Peter:

> When they had finished eating, Jesus said to Simon Peter, "Simon son of John, do you love me more than these?"
>
> "Yes, Lord," he said, "you know that I love you."
>
> Jesus said, "Feed my lambs."
>
> Again Jesus said, "Simon son of John, do you truly love me?"
>
> He answered, "Yes, Lord, you know that I love you."
>
> Jesus said, "Take care of my sheep."
>
> The third time he said to him, "Simon son of John, do you love me?"
>
> Peter was hurt because Jesus asked him the third time, "Do you love me?" He said, "Lord, you know all things; you know that I love you."
>
> Jesus said, "Feed my sheep."

When I read this story, I hear Jesus saying, "If you really do love me, go help my people. If you really love me, lend a hand to those who need it. If you really love me, assist the disadvantaged. Look after orphans and widows. Pay it forward. Do something. Serve somebody! Go! Be!"

Jesus tells Peter, "Feed my sheep." Notice that Jesus wasn't steering Peter toward inner achievement or self-improvement. Jesus wasn't focusing on Peter's talents; he was urging Peter toward the needs of others. Jesus was stressing the idea that service is not about our talents or ourselves as much as it is about how we can help others.

Clergyman Hosea Ballou said, "Preaching is to much avail, but practice is far more effective. A godly life is the strongest argument you can offer the skeptic." Each of us should have a ministry. Your Monday through Saturday should be the practice and example of your Sunday morning precepts. We need to lead by our example.

My dock supervisor at the previously mentioned Wetterau warehouse got riled up when he heard people complaining. Occasionally we received an interminable order late on our shift. We would protest, "This ain't right, man! We're supposed to be outta here in a couple hours. This'll take an entire shift!"

Our supervisor, who had to help as well, erupted with frustration. "Shut up, and get busy!" he barked, tobacco juice soaring through his visible breath on those frigid docks. Every one of us busted our butts and, nearly every time, finished that order just about the time that next shift arrived. Every single time, as we clocked out, our supervisor was the last one off the floor. I doubt many people noticed, but I did. He always made sure every man had done his part, put his things away, and cleaned up after the team following our shift. Sometimes it took him a while, but he had our backs. I respected that.

When we put others first, in the depths of our minds and in the center of our hearts, service becomes more of a natural reaction than work. In Philippians 2:1–4 (NIV), Paul writes the following:

> If you have any encouragement from being united with Christ, if any comfort from his love, if any common sharing in the Spirit, if any tenderness and compassion, then make my joy complete by being like-minded, having the same love, being one in spirit and of one mind. Do nothing out of selfish ambition or vain conceit. Rather, in humility value others above yourselves, not looking to your own interests, but each of you to the interests of others.

Go bc Jesus. Don't complain. Shut up, and get busy. If you can't serve one hundred, serve one! At a church recently, I talked to a guy who said, "I'm tired of simply hearing about Jesus. I want to see Him." When Jesus was here on Earth, sinners embraced Him and the church rejected him. The "lost" reached out to him, while the "found" demanded his crucifixion. That's because of what Jesus showed to the sinners, the seekers, and the unholy. Jesus's message was clear and constant when he was here: *Love, love, love.* People need love before the law. You have an opportunity to show them both. Go. Be. Jesus.

Call me crazy but what if we learn
To love our brothers for nothing in return?
Oh how the rules would change.

Reaching out to the ones who need help
Treating them as you first would treat yourself.
Now that would be insane.

It may just be crazy enough
To work if we could only love.
What if we somehow changed the world?
It may just be crazy enough.

~ from "Crazy Enough" by MercyMe

14

HIS WAY

Hungry for love, He looks at you. Thirsty for kindness, He begs of you. Naked for loyalty, He hopes in you. Homeless for shelter in your heart, He asks of you. Will you be that one to Him?
~ Mother Teresa

I still struggle with having the mind of a servant; I always have. My natural tendency is to think "me" first. It's just true. When I ministered in Florida, this was brought to my attention in the midst of a frank discussion with the church's senior minister. We had just left one of those elders meetings, where I was merely an observer as the sacred cows made critical decisions and weren't interested in my opinions. After all, I was the young guy. It wasn't anything personal; it was what it was. As we left the meeting, I was talking in a somewhat negative manner to our minister, Scott, about the meetings in general. Scott listened for a while and didn't say much. In his silence I only continued to yammer. At some point, Scott broke his silence and said, "You know what your problem is?" *What? My problem?* I expected him to join in with me, not combat my complaints.

"My problem?" I asked.

Then he said it. "You don't have a servant's heart." I can't imagine what it feels like to be hit in the face with a sledgehammer, but I know it couldn't feel worse than those six words did. Naturally, my defenses kicked in.

I immediately started thinking of instances when I thought Scott hadn't done a good job. I was ready to point the finger everywhere else other than at myself. "What? What are you talking about?" I asked. That was the worst thing I could have asked. For the next few minutes, Scott busted me on situation after situation when I had been selfish. Some of his statements were wrong, but the rest, like 90 percent of it, was true. As I stood there and listened, I was angry. Much like my conversation with Mr. Alligood, all those years ago in college, my ego was taking a direct hit and I didn't like it.

As I drove home, reason once again took over. Maybe Scott cared. Maybe he saw potential in me. As I look back on my relationship with Scott, despite one of the most hurtful allegations ever made about me, I know he wanted me to be more like Jesus. I was at the point where I needed what most of us need from time to time—a nice, warm slab of humble pie. I was lucky to have a friend who didn't mind serving me a slice. Over a decade later, I know one thing for sure: A servant's heart is at the core of making a difference in the lives of others. Even now, I'm sure Scott has no idea of the impact his words had on me. Now I can say it and own it: He was right, and I was wrong.

I have been lucky to be around some people whose ability to change others is evident. From what I have observed over the years, I don't really have a ten-step program to making a difference. I don't believe affecting others is about the things we do as much as it is about who we are. How do we completely change our central parts in order to become servants through and through? I think a good place to start is with that "less of me and more of you" approach. That was Jesus's purpose, and that was His way. People who really make a difference are the ones who use this mentality with God *and* with His people. What if we thought like this?

> "Less of me and more of my spouse."
> "Less of me and more my kids."
> "Less of me and more of my next door neighbor."
> "Less of me and more of my boss."
> "Less of me and more of people who rub me the wrong way."
> "Less of me and more of my church."
> "Less of me and more of that guy at work who can't stand me."
> "Less of me and more of strangers."
> "Less of me and more of a little girl in Brazil who needs me to be her sponsor."
> "Less of me and more of God."
> "Less of me and more of Jesus."

Thinking of others was Jesus's way. In the book of Acts (9:2 and 24:14), Jesus's followers are not only called Christians but are also called followers of "the Way." They didn't just have a pledge to verbalize, or a specific set of views or beliefs. They lived in a different way. Unfortunately, the Church isn't always known for it's way anymore. Political views, moral stances and intolerance of anything "secular," can sometimes become a hinderance. Ask the un-churched and you will find this is how some view people of faith. As I think back on my Bible college days, I know that some of us were more concerned about being "right" than just serving and living a life of love.

Jesus referred to himself as "the Way." In John 14:6 (NIV), Jesus says, "I am the way the truth and the life. No one comes to the Father except through me." Walking, talking, and really living His way is the ultimate apologetic and most effective discourse when attempting to lead people to Him. If you want to be Jesus to the divorced single mom on your street, offer to mow her lawn or change the oil in her car. If you want to be Jesus in your workplace, do your job as though you were working for Christ Himself. The Way is about selflessness, altruism, surrender, humility, and service.

Jesus came to serve and to inspire us to do the same, which is shown in Matthew 20:20–28 (MSG),

> It was about that time that the mother of the Zebedee brothers came with her two sons and knelt before Jesus with a request.
>
> "What do you want?" Jesus asked.
>
> She said, "Give your word that these two sons of mine will be awarded the highest places of honor in your kingdom, one at your right hand, one at your left hand."
>
> Jesus responded, "You have no idea what you're asking." And he said to James and John, "Are you capable of drinking the cup that I'm about to drink?"
>
> They said, "Sure, why not?"

> Jesus said, "Come to think of it, you are going to drink my cup. But as to awarding places of honor, that's not my business. My Father is taking care of that."
>
> When the ten others heard about this, they lost their tempers, thoroughly disgusted with the two brothers. So Jesus got them together to settle things down. He said, "You've observed how godless rulers throw their weight around, how quickly a little power goes to their heads. It's not going to be that way with you. Whoever wants to be great must become a servant. Whoever wants to be first among you must be your slave. That is what the Son of Man has done: He came to serve, not be served—and then to give away his life in exchange for the many who are held hostage."

Jesus essentially tells his friends not to worry about accolades or titles or trophies; he tells them to simply serve. Jesus tells them that giving your life for others is the epitome of greatness: "Greater love has no man than this; that a man would lay down his life for a friend." What would happen if we were to live that way?

Felipe and Donna

Felipe Garza Jr. and Donna Ashlock started dating as teenagers. They dated steadily, until Donna cooled the romance and began dating other boys. Even though Donna had cut off the relationship, the two remained close and Felipe never let his feelings for her die. While at work one day, Donna doubled over in pain, and the doctors soon discovered she was dying of degenerative heart disease. Donna's heart was enlarged, and she desperately needed a heart transplant. Felipe heard about Donna's condition and was devastated. One night, he told his mother Maria, "Mom, I love her. I'd do anything for Donna. Soon I'm going to die, and I want to give my heart to her." His mother said to herself, *Fifteen-year-olds say irrational things like this from time to time*, and she thought nothing more of it. After all, Felipe appeared to be in perfect health.

Three weeks later, Felipe woke up one morning and complained of a pain on the left side of his head. Suddenly, he lost his breath and couldn't walk. After arriving at the hospital, doctors discovered a blood vessel in Felipe's brain had burst and left him brain-dead. Felipe's situation mystified his doctors. While he remained on a respirator, his mother remembered what he had said: "I'm going to give my heart to Donna."

Felipe's family decided to let the physicians remove his heart for Donna. Later that day, doctors successfully lifted Felipe's heart from his body and placed it into Donna's chest. After the operation, Donna's father told her Felipe had evidently been sick for about three months before he died. He said, "He donated his kidneys and his eyes."

After a pause, Donna said, "And I have his heart?"

Felipe's father said, "It was something Felipe wanted to do for someone he cared for."

Felipe understood "the Way." Now, Felipe lives on in one he loves.

15

WHO DO YOU LOVE?

Love one another the way I loved you. This is the best way to love. Put your life on the line for your friends.
~ Jesus Christ

When Jesus walked this earth, he taught by the way He lived. Many people didn't understand Him. Even church officials didn't agree with His ways. Scholars of the law hated his takes on real-life issues. His disciples were often frustrated by His lessons and by His way. On rare occasions, though, some people understood. They got it. There are many times I find myself still missing the point. I look back over my life, and I see that I have often completely missed the most glaring opportunities to make an eternal difference. I deliberately chose my own comfort and happiness over the feelings and needs of others.

So, how do we make sure that we get it? Obviously, equality with God is unattainable for us. To quote a dear friend of mine, "We suck at being holy." It's true. However, we can make a conscious effort to live the way He intends for us on a more consistent basis. Jesus stressed serving. Jesus wasn't just lecturing or presenting noble ideas He would never stoop to himself. He exemplified His words in the way He lived and the way He died. Jesus showed us the way, and we have all we need within us to follow His beautiful example.

I challenge you with this question: Do you love

Jesus? This isn't Sunday school or a church class, so don't give the knee-jerk predictable answer. Do you *really* love Jesus? As a kid in church, I sang songs like "Oh, How I Love Jesus" and "My Jesus, I Love Thee," without really thinking about the lyrics. In my young dating life, I told several girls I loved them without really thinking about the meaning of those words. Certainly there are many types of love. I've said things like, "I love the Miami Dolphins," "I love Skyline Chili," and "I love The Beatles." But, realistically, I've never met any of The Beatles. I love some of their music, but I don't personally know them. I've been a Dolphins fan for over thirty-five years. I've spent excessive amounts of time watching them, reading about them, and attending many games over the years. Yet, I don't really know them either. So while I love listening to certain songs, rooting for certain teams and eating a particular type of chili with noodles and entirely too much cheese; it's not the same type of love as I have for my family. Or Jesus.

I love my wife. I'm not always the best husband, but I love her. I love her increasingly as time goes by. Over time, I've come to know and understand her more. I love my kids more than I love myself, and that's something I know is true. I love my parents very much. Jesus? Hmmm. I think I had an infatuation with Him when I first met Him. I'd say I loved Him, but I didn't really know Him. Do I *really* love Jesus? I can honestly say, "yes" now. It has taken time. I'm not the best follower. I don't represent Him well at all times. However, over time, I've come to know and understand Him more. I do love Jesus, very much.

What about you? Do you love Jesus? It is

nearly impossible to embrace "the Way" until you do. Loving Jesus is a choice. Either you do, or you don't. It's an everyday decision. It's not so unlike loving your wife or husband or boyfriend or girlfriend. What steps did you take to begin loving your significant other? What was the formula you used to begin your relationship? My guess is you took one look at him or her, and said, "Wow! That's who I want!" On the other hand, perhaps you were around him or her long enough to eventually become "wowed." I think sometimes we try to turn loving Jesus into a multiple-step formula. Do this, this, this, and this, and then you will love Jesus as He loves you. However, His love for us is not based on what we do.

Now before you throw this book into your fireplace, trash can, or your dog's mouth, allow me to clarify. Obviously there are certain things any follower of Jesus would do. One look at the Gospels and you can find tons of things Jesus finds pleasing. Forgiveness. Faith. Baptism. Prayer. Service. Mercy. Love. Sacrifice. Giving. Grace. Repentance. Loving God. Loving your neighbor. These are a few of the no-brainers. To take issue with any of them is to take issue with Christ Himself. I've had church leaders corner me on this before by saying, "What are the essentials? What are the nonnegotiables?"

To which, based on Jesus's life and theology, I'd have to say, "All of the above."

From a biblical perspective, how do you argue against repentance? How do you argue against baptism? How do you argue against mercy? We aren't going to be successful in every area of our relationship with Christ but, thankfully, salvation is not primarily about what we do. Rather, at the foundation of our hope are things like God's grace and Jesus's blood. Our faith in God's Word and Jesus's promises are the essentials, not church attendance pins or man's approval or theological degrees. It doesn't take too much time spent with Jesus before we have to say, "Wow! That's who I want!" It is within the confines of that "wow" that we can truly become what He wants. Christians. Difference makers. Servants.

I once heard a sermon that left me know everything the speaker was against and little, if anything, that he was for. The time for petitions and protests are over. It's up to every person who professes Jesus as Lord to initiate a personal revolution. The world will be convinced Jesus is the best option when Christianity produces the very best individuals. If you want to change some opinions, then really love your neighbor as you love yourself. Demonstrate tenderhearted mercy and kindness toward others. If you really want to make a difference, feed the hungry. Visit those in prison, and show them that their minds and souls are free. Provide a home for the homeless. Look after orphans and widows so they know they are not defined by labels. Sponsor or adopt a child. Care for the sick, and watch what true love does in terms of emotional health. These are the essentials.

Consider Jesus's words in Matthew 25:31–40 (MSG):

> When he finally arrives, blazing in beauty and all his angels with him, the Son of Man will take his place on his glorious throne. Then all

> the nations will be arranged before him and he will sort the people out, much as a shepherd sorts out sheep and goats, putting sheep to his right and goats to his left.
>
> Then the King will say to those on his right, "Enter, you who are blessed by my Father! Take what's coming to you in this kingdom. It's been ready for you since the world's foundation. And here's why:
>
> I was hungry and you fed me,
> I was thirsty and you gave me a drink,
> I was homeless and you gave me a room,
> I was shivering and you gave me clothes,
> I was sick and you stopped to visit,
> I was in prison and you came to me."
>
> Then those "sheep" are going to say, "Master, what are you talking about? When did we ever see you hungry and feed you, thirsty and give you a drink? And when did we ever see you sick or in prison and come to you?" Then the King will say, "I'm telling the solemn truth: Whenever you did one of these things to someone overlooked or ignored, that was me—you did it to me."

Jesus is once again talking about the greatness of serving all of mankind. The way to heaven is not through ceremonies or formulas or man-made traditions and legalistic banter. Jesus said, "I am the Way." He also said, "No one comes to the Father except through me." It's not about our religion or knowledge. It's not about work either.

What? Isn't that contrary to the whole serving thing? That depends on your heart. I don't do nice things to prove I love my wife or my kids. I don't have to. I do nice things for my family because of my love for them. Because I love them, I want to please them. I desire their happiness and welfare. Nothing you do will make Jesus love you more than He already does. Remember, he resurrected for you two thousand years before you whimpered your first sound. If you really love Jesus, genuinely love Him, your service will be a natural act because of that love. You will love others because of your love for Jesus. The more time you spend together, the more like Him you'll likely become. It's about humility. It's about love. Who do *you* love?

16

THE RIPPLE EFFECT

Blessed is the influence of one true, loving human soul on another.
~ George Eliot, novelist

You have an effect on everyone you meet and know. Jesus influenced the masses in His own day in three short years—people like the woman at the well, the blind, the crippled, the disciples (none of which were ministers or hired clergy), prostitutes, lepers, the thief on the cross, tax collectors, and tons of "sinners" in general. Jesus had a special ability with those who were deemed by others as unholy or lacking spirituality. Jesus wasn't condescending, judgmental, hateful, or rude. Jesus usually served the people He touched and then spoke the truth to them.

Just like Jesus or your minister or anyone who is effective in sharing the message of Christ, we each can influence the people we meet. And the people we meet and serve can impact us as well. We all have opportunities to encourage and inspire those around us every day. Our failure to do so can have devastating results for those whose salvation depends on our mercy, love, and depiction of who Jesus really is and what He can do in our lives. I know this all too well. I want to share with you a true story that took place in my life. You might find it hard to believe. I have changed the names of those involved, in case any of their friends or family read this. I am not proud of this story, but it is true. It broke my heart and changed my attitude about loving others.

1981

I was a seventh-grader at E. Russell Hicks Middle School in Hagerstown, Maryland. I wasn't much different from my classmates. I was trying to figure out my ever-changing body and complexion, learning how to talk to girls and how to fight, and being cruel to everyone who wasn't like my group of friends. Being cruel is something seventh-graders are great at, and as much as I hate to admit this, when it came to immature cuts and juvenile cruelty, I was an all-star. One of the worst things I was ever part of was something we all called "the money pit." Suffice to say, I don't look forward to talking to God about this one.

In our lunchroom, there were rows of tables where we ate each day. All of us ate there, except the kids who didn't have lunch or couldn't afford lunch. Those kids always sat in "the money pit." It was a smaller triangular area encased by four or five steps that dug into the ground in front of a stage. It was like an orchestra pit. Every day, the same cast assembled down there. The Dempsey twins, Carlos Brisbane, Jimmy Baxter, Brian White, and of course, Daphne Simpson. Daphne was poor, dirty, socially inept, and poorly dressed. My friends and I always took our change and tossed it into "the money pit" just to watch these poor kids fight for the money. I kid you not. It was downright despicable. I hate that I did that, but I did.

Daphne got much more from me and my

classmates. Her thick-frame glasses, broken speech, and strange scent were all the ammunition we needed. We treated her horribly. That girl was sucker punched, was hit in the back of the head with rocks, had her glasses broken, was provoked into fights (which were never fair), and was decorated with "Kick Me" signs on a daily basis. I never physically harmed her, but I think my words were probably more hurtful than the fists, feet, and rocks that regularly struck her. I was the polar opposite of Jesus. I wasn't acting as a Christian. I'd gone to church, heard about Jesus, and had even been baptized at a young age. I knew better—I just didn't know Jesus. Daphne certainly did not see a glimpse of Him in me. I did not fully understand the ripple effect of my detestable behavior and failure to be like Jesus to Daphne…until years later.

2000

When my parents announced they were taking in a foster child, I wasn't overly surprised. Growing up I always had foster brothers and sisters. Mom and Dad took in kids every several months until the children's parents were able to provide care for them again or until the children's legal adoption by another family. I was in student ministry in Florida when my parents called me. "How would you like to have a sister?" Mom asked. I always wanted a sister.

"You're not pregnant, are you, Mom?" I said to my fifty-something mother. She told me they wanted my approval before bringing Molly home. I assured them that I thought it would be awesome. They proceeded, and I was excited to come home for

Christmas with some gifts for my new sister.

I came through the front door, greeted first by my new twelve-year-old sister. She gave me a strong hug around the waist and displayed all the giddy excitement of an agitated Jack Russell Terrier. We had a great day, exchanged gifts, and had dinner. That night Molly said, "I hear you went to South High."

"Yeah, I did," I told Molly.

She asked, "When did you go there?"

I said, "I was there from '83 till '86, when I graduated."

Molly's demeanor became eager. She said, "I'll bet you knew my mom then."

I was instantly intrigued. "Your mom went to South High?"

"Yep," she said, "until '84."

"What's her name?" I asked.

Have you ever ordered a sweet tea only to receive a Diet Coke instead? It's especially nasty when you hate diet sodas. You expect sweet, sugary refreshment, and instead, you get a gross combination of carbonated licorice and goat urine. (That's what's *really* in a Diet Coke, by the way.) Molly's next few words were a lot like that. "Daphne Simpson," she said. "Did you know her? Were you guys friends?" Molly's words were like daggers. Each one stabbed my memory and brought back all of the horrible things I had said and done to Daphne.

What could I say? All I could muster was, "Oh, yeah, I knew her, just not very well. She was always nice to me." That was all the truth I could release.

Molly said, "I don't know her that well either. She has a lot of problems. Nobody can ever seem to help her. I wish someone could. She's my mom, and I love her anyway."

I went into my parents' bathroom with a mix of heartache, shame, and nausea. To know that I was part of a ruined life and that I never helped was bad enough. Now I was calling Daphne's offspring my sister, and attempting to show her love made me feel like a big, insincere phony. Molly knew I worked in the church and that I was a Christian. I knew she would have future visits with her mom back at the agency and wondered how that conversation would go. Molly would say, "My new brother is a minister and a good Christian guy. You went to school with him, Mom. Do you remember Tony Wolf?"

Then Daphne would say, "Oh, you mean the same Tony Wolf who used to call me nasty names, throw change at me, and laugh when people were kicking me? That Tony Wolf? He's a minister? So that's what Christians are like, huh?"

After that, I thought, *Who else have I treated terribly in my life? Who else have I destroyed with my comments? Is there anyone I should treat better now?* I felt so awful. How could anyone treat someone the way I treated Daphne and all the others? I never realized how much of an effect I could have on people or how that would change them or those around them. Maybe being nice to Daphne wouldn't have improved her life situation, but she certainly would've seen Christians differently…and so would her daughter.

As I get older, I can't stress enough how important it is to make the most of every chance to touch others in a positive way. Paul gave this same advice to the church in Colosse, in Colossians 4:5

(NIV) when he writes, "Be wise in the way you act toward outsiders; make the most of every opportunity." You never know whom you are going to meet or where they are in life. You never know when you are going to sit down next to someone who has a serious need. You never know when you are going to stand in line with someone who is wrestling with his or her faith.

One thing is certain: Every day we encounter His people, and we have unlimited opportunities. What you do, what you say, and how you treat people makes a difference. My wish for you is that it is a positive one. My will is that you can plant seeds or water those that are already there. I hope that when you lie down in a bed for the last time, you have cared for many. I hope that when you're breathing your last breaths, you know you did as much for others as you could have. I hope you feel content and that you can smile. I hope you can mull over your years and see how much you have changed for the better and how often you served others.

I once read an old mystic proverb about making a positive difference. The mystic said, "I was a revolutionary when I was young and all my prayer to God was: 'Lord, give me the energy to change the world.' As I approached middle age and realized that my life was half gone without my changing a single soul, I changed my prayer to: 'Lord, give me the grace to change all those who come into contact with me, just my family and friends, and I shall be satisfied.' Now that I am an old man and my days are numbered, I have begun to see how foolish I have been. My one prayer now is: 'Lord, give me the grace to change myself.' If I had prayed for this right from the start, I would not have wasted my life."

The mystic gets it. Our individual legacies are closely tied to our willingness to work on ourselves. Each time we selflessly reach out and serve another person, there is change. There is change in those we serve and in ourselves. A ripple effect starts from within, as individuals, as we understand and embrace God's will for our lives.

17

SERVE ONE

We only have what we give.
~ Isabelle Allende, Author

Gene Woolard was one of my favorite people my last couple of years at college. He was one of the only students who faithfully attended every basketball game. At home games, we had a smattering of fans from the other teams. A few of our professors, our coach's wife, and our girlfriends made up our fan base, usually about twenty-one fans. Nonetheless, almost without fail, Gene was in the stands. Going back to the dorm after games and talking to Gene was always like having my own ESPN analyst to break down our performance. He pointed to things like missed free throws and turnovers, but he also always told me he liked my effort and attitude, even when we lost miserably.

Gene and I talked during a recent visit to his church. He told me his church was struggling. He told me he had received offers to go to other churches in recent years, but he felt he was supposed to stay and serve the people God gave him: "For whatever reason, God wants me to serve these folks. We are really struggling. I have had some other offers that would be more beneficial to my family. But God keeps telling me to serve here." I was truly inspired. Gene knows it isn't about bigger churches or better opportunities; it's about the ones God puts in front of you today, right where you are. Then Gene told me something I never knew.

"I was in the military before I came to Bible college. They don't call it 'the service' for nothing. I really learned what sacrifice and putting others first was all about in the army. When I headed into the ministry, service was all I knew. It was what I respected. I was all set to go to another college, but I had told someone from my church I would at least go check out Roanoke [now MACU]," Gene said. "My father and I made the trip out to eastern North Carolina and pulled up on the street in front of MACU. When we got out, we saw a man painting an older building behind the chapel. We walked over to ask him where to go, and before long, we were all standing there, painting, laughing, sweating, and talking together. An hour later, he directed us inside to admissions. As he opened the door for us, I said, 'It was great talking with you; what was your name?' He said, 'Oh, I'm Bill Griffin. I'm the president here.'" Gene continued, "When I saw the president outside painting an old building in the summer heat, I knew that this was the place for me."

How many of us would really do that kind of thing? Think about it. You are the president of the college. Wouldn't you just hire someone to do that? Hearing that story reminded me of my junior year, when I saw Bill Griffin's predecessor, former President George Bondurant cleaning windows on the third floor of our unfinished dorm. Drywall dust, dirt, and sweat covered his old bib coveralls and painters' cap. President Bondurant was retired. He founded Roanoke Bible College (MACU) in 1948, and with all due respect, he had to have been at least 125 years old.

Nevertheless, there he was, a retired, elderly college founder and former president. A man who had started several colleges and many churches was doing what he apparently had done his whole life. He was serving.

Bill Griffin changed Gene Woolard's life. He didn't do it with a well-researched sermon or philosophical advice. He didn't give Gene a big, fat check or direct him to a financial planner. He didn't sing him a song. Bill Griffin changed Gene's life with a paintbrush, some perspiration, and a servant's heart. Bill Griffin served one that day.

Joy is found in serving others. God gave you an indescribable gift when He created you. Jesus valued you so much that He died and resurrected for you. He has a purpose for your life, and He wants you to use the ability He has given you. He wants you to serve. He wants to impact others through your obedience. He knows that with His help, you are capable of all things. All things are possible, and you don't have to have a master's degree in theology to do it. Jesus's impact occurred through serving. That is where your gifts will work in ways beyond your imagination.

He hand-painted you, sculpted you, and supplied you with a case of talents of which only He knows the depths and extents. When I was in high school, I received an invitation to attend a vocational school for artists for the duration of my junior and senior years. While I was there, I studied from a book called *Drawing on the Right Side of the Brain* by Dr. Betty Edwards. Without getting into the physical and mental aspects and theories of the book, the exercises we performed from it provided amazing results. Some students were there for their gifts in photography, others to be architects and some fashion designers. My skills were in cartooning and portrait artwork. Every student improved in unbelievable fashion over the few weeks as we went through the book and its exercises. By the end of the course, classmates who admitted, "I can't draw stick figures," were drawing about as well as I could before we started the book. We are all capable of a lot more than we think.

We are sort of like ten-speed bicycles. Some of us just coast through life. Most of us have gears we never even use. Renaissance artist Michelangelo once prayed, "Lord, let me always desire more than I think I can do." He also once claimed that masterpieces are all around us—we only have to chisel away at the rough edges to discover them. I see masterpieces all the time. I'm not referring to art; I'm talking about people.

I have recorded music projects over the years with an incredible producer and engineer. He has worked with or been connected to some of the biggest names in the industry, but you would never, ever know it. He's humble, welcoming, and as genuine as they come, and his faith is evident in his life. He is the kind of man I hope my daughters will marry someday. With the highest respect to his incredible craft, David Browning is a far greater person than he is a musician.

I met a young man named Richmond Wandera at a Compassion function in Nashville. Richmond is from Uganda and was once a sponsored child. He flourished under that sponsorship, found his way to the United States, got a degree in theology, and returned to his homeland to plant churches and oversee many ministries throughout his East African country. Richmond was rescued from poverty and returned to his home to tell his people about Jesus.

A dear friend who passed away a few years ago, Tom, was one of the most generous men I've ever met. Tom was a knee specialist, and he was an elder in his church.

One of the greatest Christians I've ever known, Ralph, worked for Siemens for most of his adult life while leading everyone around him by his example. Ralph showed me Jesus every time I saw him, by the way he lived.

One of my neighbor friends, Jeff, has a lucrative crane-and-hoist business that allows him to fund mission trips and other substantial needs of his congregation. Jeff also plays drums in the praise band at his church.

My old friends Mark Lukhard and Jeff Kennedy are still introducing people to Jesus in very different arenas. By the way, Jeff, is the same Dr. Jeff Kennedy who wrote the introduction for this book.

My old youth minister, Jay, is teaching character education in public schools.

The Gettigs are still nursing, teaching, fighting fires, and going to camp.

And somewhere in eastern North Carolina, old man Alligood is still out there on a lawn mower…and still molding people's lives.

All of these people have one thing in common: They love Jesus. They all use, in a positive way, the gifts and passions God has given them. Most of the time, as you can see, that translates into serving on some level or another.

Be passionate about what you do every day.

Abraham Lincoln once said, "Whatever you are, be a good one." That means if you are a cook, prepare the best dishes you can. If you're in construction, work each job as if you are building your own home. If you're a teacher, remember you are instructing and molding God's children. Do each job like Jesus is your boss and God is the owner. In Colossians 3:23–24 (NIV), Paul tells the Colossians, "Whatever you do, work at it with all your heart, as working for the Lord, not for human masters, since you know that you will receive an inheritance from the Lord as a reward. It is the Lord Christ you are serving." Strive to do the best you can, from where you are, daily. Don't look past the amazing opportunities surrounding you right now. God will bless you and decide when and where and what's next.

At the same time, be passionate about where God has gifted you and obedient to what He desires from you. He wouldn't have given you your specific gifts if He didn't have something specific for you to do with them. That would be like giving your mom a football helmet to wear on her birthday. Unless your mom plays for the Indianapolis Colts, why would you do such a thing? You wouldn't take a chainsaw to a baby shower, would you? You wouldn't buy your great grandma a surfboard, would you? We usually try to give people things that are useful or that they enjoy. Your Father is no different. God has given us each abilities that are extremely useful to us. Strive to utilize them and sharpen them. If you have a talent for painting but you're a broker, don't leave your easel in the closet. Use the weekends, or an hour or so at night, to enjoy your gift and develop your skills. You never know when God might want to employ your expertise. The worst thing you can do is bury the talents He has entrusted to you. The best you can do is hone and share them.

The Parable of the Eagle and the Chicken

There once was an Eagle and a Chicken. The two were very close and spent much of their time flying together. One day, while high in the sky, the Chicken said to the Eagle, "Man, I'm starving! Let's go get some grub!"

"Oh yeah, you can count me in," said the Eagle. So the two zeroed in on some animals eating in a pasture and decided to check it out.

When they hit the ground and started eating, a nearby Cow said, "Hey, guys, come get some of this corn—it's awesome!"

The two birds were shocked that the Cow wanted to share. "You want to share with us?" asked the Eagle.

"Why not?" said the Cow. "When it's all gone, Farmer Fran will just give us more." Given this information, they all feasted until the corn was gone.

"Farmer Fran must be a nice guy," said the Chicken.

"Oh, he is! And since he grows all of our food, we don't even have to work for it!" said the Cow.

"All right, hold up," said the Chicken. "You mean to tell me he just gives it to you?"

"Yep," said the Cow, "and, better than that, he even gives us a place to live too!"

The Eagle and Chicken just looked at each

other with their beaks agape in disbelief. They had always had to work hard for food and shelter. The Chicken looked at the Eagle and said, "Man, we get all the food we want without working and a nice barn that's warm and dry? I've worked my tail off for years. I'm staying. That's all there is to it—I'm staying."

"Listen, Chicken," said the Eagle. "Doesn't this seem a little too good to be true? I mean, I've always been told nothing worth having is free of charge. Plus, I like flying high and free. Finding food and shelter isn't so bad. I actually like the challenge." Nevertheless, the Chicken stayed even while his dear friend, the Eagle, soared away. Time went by, and the Chicken was living large. He ate as much as he wanted, when he wanted, as often as he wanted. He enjoyed free accommodations, and he never worked.

One day he heard Farmer Fran tell his wife, Frieda, he wanted some fried chicken for dinner. The Chicken finally put it all together and realized what was about to happen. He knew he had better fly away, as the Eagle had months before. However, when he attempted to fly, he found he had grown too fat and lazy. In a matter of hours, he was headless on a plate next to some mashed potatoes and green beans.

When you give up life's challenges in pursuit of "security," you might give up your freedom. In addition, if you don't use your gifts, you might lose them.

Gifts Are in the Present

There might even be gifts you have yet to discover but that will come about by simply looking for them. I mentioned painting earlier. Anna Mary Moses, better known as "Grandma Moses," never painted until she was seventy-eight years old! Yet she managed to paint over sixteen hundred pieces of art during her last twenty-three years of life. That's almost two paintings a day! Her works became critically commended and brought honors from US presidents.

Connie Madigan, a defenseman for the 1972–73 Saint Louis Blues professional hockey team, holds a record that might never be broken. At age thirty-eight, the rugged defender became the oldest "rookie" to make his NHL debut when he took the ice on February 1, 1973, against the Montreal Canadiens.

Harland Sanders cooked chicken dinners for people at his service station in Corbin, Kentucky, for years. It wasn't until the young age of sixty-two that he founded his legendary restaurant, Kentucky Fried Chicken.

It's never too late or too early to use your gifts in amazing ways. You are capable of astounding feats when you use your God-given gifts, so be willing to try to stretch your abilities. An old quote says, "Never be afraid to do something new. Remember, amateurs built the ark; professionals built the *Titanic*." Leap from the boat. Focus. Walk on water.

Ultimately, how you use your gifts to serve and love others is your legacy. You decide each day how you interact with others. Do you use your time and abilities to serve a higher purpose or drop them into the ground hidden from sight or use? Do you diligently approach every opportunity as though you are working for a holy boss, or are you lazy and unwilling to fly when it comes to soaring to the heights

He created for you? Do you love or just talk about love? Remember, in Ephesians 3:20 (MSG) Paul wrote, "God can do anything, you know—far more than you could ever imagine or guess or request in your wildest dreams! He does it not by pushing us around but by working within us, his Spirit deeply and gently within us."

The secret to creating authentic joy in your life is to serve, give, and express love to others. In the words of music legend Paul McCartney, "And in the end, the love you take is equal to the love you make."

Actor Leonard Nimoy put it this way: "The miracle is this—the more we share, the more we have." What you get usually equals what you give. Since the extent of your love is completely up to you, you already have the key to your own happiness and fulfillment. What remains is for you to determine what you do with your key. Just remember who gave it to you.

My life's most fulfilling moments were those spent helping others. From feeding my baby girls oatmeal to cutting up trees in Pass Christian to holding the hands of dying friends and acquaintances, I am finding my place in this world. I pray for that same clarity for you. I pray that God grants you wisdom and strength as you learn, by trial and error and in elation and grief, to live a life of love. We are to show "the Way" by how we serve and how we love others.

Serve one God. Serve His people. In this service, there is eternal joy to be experienced. If you can't serve one hundred, serve one.

ABOUT THE AUTHOR

An established national speaker, comedian, musician and author, Tony Wolf is a multi-talented artist who engages and entertains people of all ages with his cross-generational approach. Tony's gifts in music and communication have carried him to 44 states on stages with Skillet, Mercy Me, DC Talk, Audio Adrenaline, KJ-52, Sanctus Real, JJ Heller, Superchick, Newsboys, Josh McDowell, Mike Singletary, For King and Country, Rich Mullins, Toby Mac, Third Day, Jeremy Camp, Kutless, Matt Maher, Britt Nicole, Josh Wilson, Family Force 5, Guy Penrod, Royal Tailor, Kari Jobe, Bread Of Stone, Rapture Ruckus, Switchfoot, Andy Mineo, Citizen Way, Michael W. Smith, Chonda Pierce, Natalie Grant, Mandisa and Rebecca St. James among others.

Tony is a veteran of ministry and a SCORRE certified dynamic speaker. Tony graduated from MACU with a degree in Counseling and was ordained in 1993. He has since authored books, produced music projects and has been involved in various outreach endeavors including a mission to help Katrina victims with Campus Crusade for Christ in Pass Christian, Mississippi. Tony is a voice and advocate for Compassion International and has helped rescue over 15,000 children from poverty. Tony uses a combination of creativity, humor and passion that is peerless and unmatched. Tony lives in Westfield, Indiana with his wife Laura, three daughters Brooklyn, Katie and Adrienne and son Jude.

You can connect with Tony in the following ways:

www.tonywolf.com
facebook.com/thattonywolfguy
twitter@thattonwolfguy
Instagram: thattonwolfguy

39899514R00091

Made in the USA
Middletown, DE
28 January 2017